The aim of this book is to help promote a more complete physical education, based on an understanding of the body and how it works, and to help an individual maximise their physi... potential – to go for their own personal 'gold'.

Modern physical education, as taught in most schools, tends to encourage the practice of sports and games and yet gives little instruction on their immediate and long term effect on the body. It provides for those who excel in goal orientated activities, giving little or no encouragement to the less competitive, physically weaker, underdeveloped or disabled child and young adult.

Designed for use at home, in schools and colleges, the approximate age range at which GOING FOR GOLD is directed is between 10 and 16 years, with its emphasis not on competitive exercise and sport but on individually oriented exercise, the complementing of various activities ie. the intensity of weight lifting and its physical benefits with, for example, the additional relaxing benefits of yoga, and finally the pleasure and enjoyment that can be gained at any level from team games.

By providing a comprehensive look at the body: how it works, how its stamina, suppleness, co-ordination, strength and flexibility can be maximised, GOING FOR GOLD will help improve and enhance the attributes of a healthy body that are so vital to the successful practice of any physical activity.

Illustrated throughout with specially commissioned photographs featuring Daley Thompson working and demonstrating exercises and sports with children and young adults, GOING FOR GOLD is an exciting, attractive and practical guide to a lifetime of health and fitness.

Other titles by Peter Walker
& published by Unwin Paperbacks.

Baby Gymnastics (with Arthur Balaskas)
Baby Relax

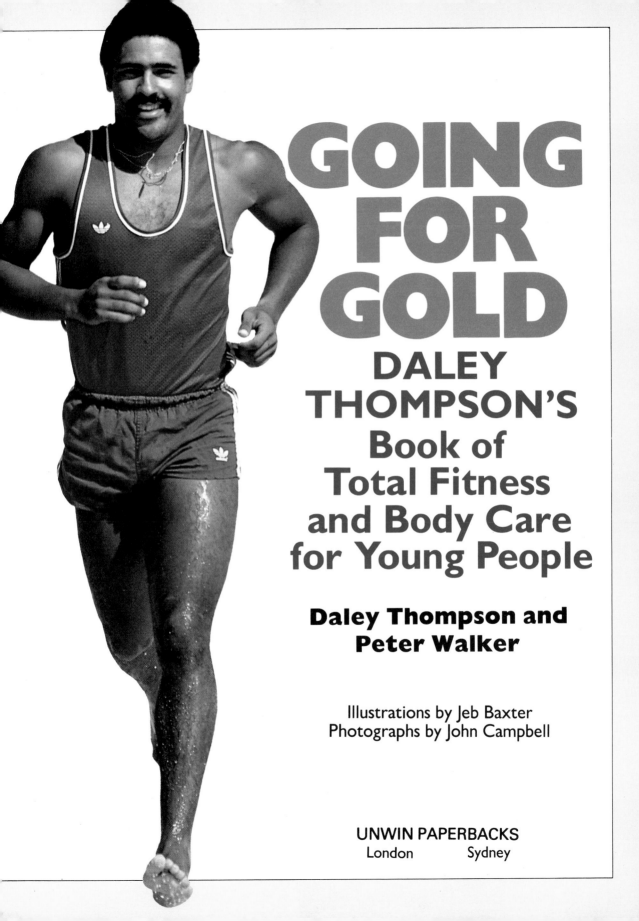

GOING FOR GOLD

DALEY THOMPSON'S
Book of
Total Fitness
and Body Care
for Young People

**Daley Thompson and
Peter Walker**

Illustrations by Jeb Baxter
Photographs by John Campbell

UNWIN PAPERBACKS
London   Sydney

First published in Great Britain by Unwin® Paperbacks,
an imprint of Unwin Hyman Limited, in 1987

UNWIN HYMAN LIMITED
Denmark House, 37–39 Queen Elizabeth Street,
London SE1 2QB
and
40 Museum Street, London WC1A 1LU

Allen & Unwin Australia Pty Ltd
8 Napier Street, North Sydney, NSW 2060, Australia

Allen & Unwin New Zealand Ltd with the Port Nicholson Press,
60 Cambridge Terrace,
Wellington, New Zealand

British Library Cataloguing in Publication Data
Thompson, Daley
   Going for gold: Daley Thompson's book of
   total fitness and body care for young
   people.
   1. Youth—Health and hygiene
   I. Title   II. Walker, Peter, 1942–
   613'.024055   RA564.5

ISBN 0–04–613070–5

Typeset by Keyboard Services, Luton
Printed by W. S. Cowell Ltd., Ipswich
Book and cover design by The Pinpoint Design Company

Contents

Acknowledgements   8

Foreword by Daley Thompson   9

1 Why Exercise?   11
Physical development 11
Emotional development 11
A balance 13

2 The Body   14
Musculoskeletal system 14
Skeleton · Joints · Muscles · The importance of exercise
Respiratory system 22
Breathing · Good posture · Maximum efficiency ·
Benefits of abdominal breathing
Heart and circulation 23
The blood · The heart · The circulatory system ·
The aerobic process · The anaerobic process
Digestion 26
The food you eat · Exercise and digestion
The nervous system 28
The brain · The spinal cord · The autonomic nervous system ·
Integration and learning · Nervous disorders · Exercise
and the nervous system
The endocrine system 30
Pituitary · Thyroid · Parathyroids · Thymus · Adrenals · Pancreas ·
The sex glands · The endocrine and nervous systems
Youthfulness and age 31
Youth · Age

3 You Are What You Eat   33
Nutrients 33
Proteins · Carbohydrates · Fats · Vitamins · Minerals · Fibre · Water
Recommended foods and proportions 34
Whole grains · Animal foods · Fruit and vegetables · Salad
and cooking oils and fatty spreads · Highly processed foods
Good eating habits 37
Exercise and nutrition 37
Useful tips

4 Common Complaints and Their Treatment · 38

Obesity 38
Treatment
Acne 38
Treatment
Anaemia 39
Treatment
Fainting and giddiness 40
Treatment
Dental decay 40
Treatment
Stress 41
Recognising stress · The effects of stress · Causes and cures

5 Exercise · 43

Dynamic and static exercise 43
Static exercise · Dynamic exercise

6 Relaxation and Breathing · 46

Relaxation 46
Relaxation technique
Breathing and relaxation 47
Breathing technique

7 Static Exercise Programme · 48

Ankles 49
Ankles and knees 51
Hips 54
Shoulders and spine 62
Head and neck 66

8 Yoga and T'ai Chi · 70

Yoga 70
Hatha yoga · Pranayama · Meditation · Going Further
T'ai chi chuan 71
Chi
Flexibility and strength

9 Manipulation · 73

Head and neck 74
Shoulders and spine 76
Hips, legs and pelvic floor 82

10 Popular Sports Today   90

Why dynamic exercise?   90
Your body, your self · Benefits of dynamic exercise
Jogging, running and sprinting   92
The mechanics of running · A warning!
Gymnastics   93
The floor exercises · The apparatus
Weight training   96
Scientific weightlifting
Swimming   98
Useful tips · Benefits of swimming
Cycling   100
Cycling today · Useful tips · Benefits of cycling
Roller skating   102
Useful tips · Benefits of roller skating
Ice skating   104
Useful tips · Benefits of ice skating
Skiing   106
Skiing today · Useful tips
Football   108
Football today · Footballing skills · Warming up · Benefits
Tennis   110
Tennis yesterday and today · Useful tips · Warming up · Mental training
Squash   112
The need for fitness · Warming up and training
Cricket   114
Useful tips
Basketball   116
Useful tips · Warming up and Training
Baseball   118
The pitch · The game · Special skills
American Football   120
The basics · The players · Scoring · Playing · Special considerations

11 Injuries During Exercise   122

Ligaments   122
Method of treatment
Muscles   123
Sprains and strains, *Method of treatment*
Cramps and spasms, *Method of treatment*
Inflammation   124
Recovery

Appendix 1 Further Reading   125

Appendix 2 Useful Addresses   126

Acknowledgements

The authors and publishers would like to thank the following people for their help with the book.

From Holland Park Comprehensive School, Maggie Pringle (Head-teacher); staff members of the P.E. department: Norman Holmes, Niall Whelan, Anne Allen, Sue Thwaites and Peter Rattigan; the following pupils: Gwenny Whelan, Surendra Premji, Audrey Chakaodza, Roxana Kennedy, Hetty Kovach, Warren Exell, Finn Connolly, Nebina Aman, Donna Bizzell, Kate Read, Esther Barry, Marcel Atteen, Simon Kane, Courtney Shorter-Taylor, Jim Futcher, George Gardiner, Van Man Doan, Sarah Stevens, Phong Tran, Dominic Brennan, Noe Seudas and Simon Corbett.

From The Young Place, Iris Tomlinson and Chris Harrison-Kerr, Maxine Bunting, Clarissa Millar, Emily Benson, Joanna Sutherland, Matthew Conway and Evan Williams.

In addition we would also like to thank Adidas U.K. for supplying equipment; Uxbridge Cricket Club; The Fulham Cardinals; and Sarah Stirk, Nathan Davis, Jacob Corke, Candice Marks, Joy Broadway, Fiona Schutzmann.

Finally, thanks are also due to John Campbell for the photographs, Jeb Baxter for the illustrations and All-Sport Agency and Zeta Picture Library for the additional photos.

Foreword by Daley Thompson

In trying to pass on the benefits of experience to the developing mind, I won't be the first to emphasise that a positive dictum is received more readily, and acted upon more effectively, than a negative one. This is of course vital when it comes to saying 'don't smoke, don't sniff glue' or 'don't take drugs'.

I believe it may be of real value to introduce a more positive note into my continuous support of any movement which will prevent such abuse of the body, one's loved ones and the environment. Thus my collaboration with Peter Walker is to help in filling those low periods, when my younger friends are most susceptible to the vaunted delights of drugs, be they nicotine, alcohol or cocaine, with the even more satisfying delights of increasing one's self-respect and personal well being.

The contents of this book represent a positive step towards achievement, fulfilling a need which is instilled in us from babyhood, but for many of today's young people may never be found through work.

Young people are of course especially gregarious and, in addition to individual achievement, getting together to exercise or compete through sporting activities is fun. They will be mentally more resilient to harm and they will enjoy it. I hope you will too.

Daley Thompson

1 Why Exercise?

Adolescence – the period between about 10 years and 18 – is one of the most important and exciting times of your life. It is a time of rapid physical development and growth and emotional adjustment, reflecting your change from childhood to adult maturity. But, it is also a vulnerable and impressionable time, and your ability to cope successfully during these changes will affect you well into your adult life.

Physical development

It is at this time, with the rapid increase in muscle power, that future athletes, gymnasts, dancers and sportsmen and women become apparent. And, it is at this time, much more so than during adulthood, that you can sow the seeds of health and fitness, when you can drastically improve your body's shape, performance and potential.

Your development is activated by the endocrine glands, releasing various hormones that set in train a complex series of physical and emotional changes that affect the way you look, think and behave. Your height and weight increase, your nervous system matures, your coordination improves, and the size of your lungs and heart increases, the heart nearly doubling in size. Because of this improvement in physical capacity, there are also changes in your biological rhythms and patterns. For example your body begins to use less energy to sustain itself – your basal metabolic rate drops.

This physical development will obviously allow you to improve your sporting capabilities. However, whether you like to dance, skate, run, cycle, ski, or merely wish to lead a healthy active life, unless your body has strength, flexibility and stamina you will be severely hampered. It is these three attributes that are stressed in this book – the even development of them is the foundation of health and fitness. Whatever activity you wish to excel in, it must work on your strength, flexibility and stamina or be combined with another activity or pastime that balances these capacities.

Emotional development

Throughout history, from the ancient Greeks and Romans through the Renaissance, physical excellence and mental and emotional maturity have always gone hand in hand. This may seem difficult to achieve during adolescence. The change from child to adult can often be confusing and isolating, and certainly creates periods of emotional strain. Changes of mood, a desire for non-conformity and inconsistency in developing relationships is common and often bewilders adults, who rapidly seem to forget the trials and tribulations they went through during adolescence.

Normally every individual goes through three phases of sexual interest as they grow up. The first is known as the autosexual phase, when interest

centres on your own body and sexual interests. Then comes the homosexual phase, when emotional attachments are formed with members of the same sex. And finally there is the heterosexual phase, in which interests and activities are shared with members of the opposite sex. However, this awakening sexual awareness and the radical alterations in the shape and size of the body are often accompanied by periods of shyness and even clumsiness. Furthermore, the early development of girls and later development of boys often separates friends from each other and exaggerates the feelings of awkwardness.

Exercise and physical activity can play a powerful role in helping people through this period of rapid development, and often provides an excellent opportunity to mix with other people, at a time when such socialising might otherwise seem difficult. Worries about the nature and speed of development and immature emotional obsessions are forgotten about and, as the body strengthens, self-doubt gives way to self-confidence.

A balance

This book will hopefully show you some of the immediate and long-term benefits of different sports, games and exercises, allowing you to choose the ones that you enjoy and that might help you to balance your body's development and performance. Such a regular programme of exercise will relax your mind and give your body those three magic ingredients – strength, flexibility and stamina.

You will then stand a much better chance of being mentally *and* physically alert and adept, free from mental exhaustion and bubbling over with natural exuberance.

2 The Body

When does one and one equal one? At conception, when a reproductive cell from each parent merges into a single cell. The human body subsequently develops from this single cell, entailing billions of cell divisions, with each individual cell retaining all the major features of a living organism.

Grouped together into layers, the cells form tissues. These tissues in turn are arranged into organs that perform specialised functions; for convenience these organs and their functions are referred to as systems. For example, the body is supported by the skeletal system, moved by the muscular system and controlled by the nervous system. Life and activity is maintained with energy obtained from food ingested through the digestive system and oxygen obtained through the respiratory system. These ingredients are distributed by the blood vascular system, which also helps to remove wastes to the urinary system. Physical and chemical processes are integrated by the endocrine system, and the species is reproduced by the reproductive system.

Musculoskeletal system

The musculoskeletal system is the overall term for the muscles, bones and joints that function together to protect, position and move the body through space. These are the most obvious parts of the human body and together they constitute some three-quarters of its total mass and weight.

Skeleton

The skeleton consists of bones and joints and is the basis of the body's form and structure. The skeleton provides a living, moving, supporting frame for the soft parts of the body. It protects vital organs within its frame, like the heart and lungs within the rib cage and the brain and spinal cord within the spine and skull. The bones themselves provide a major reservoir into which calcium is deposited and from which it is withdrawn as needed. Within the bones takes place the formation of red blood cells, vital to the life and growth of all the body's tissues and organs.

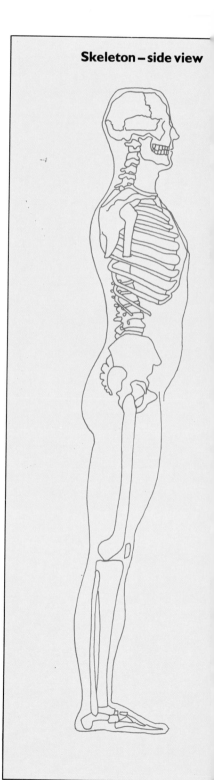

Skeleton – side view

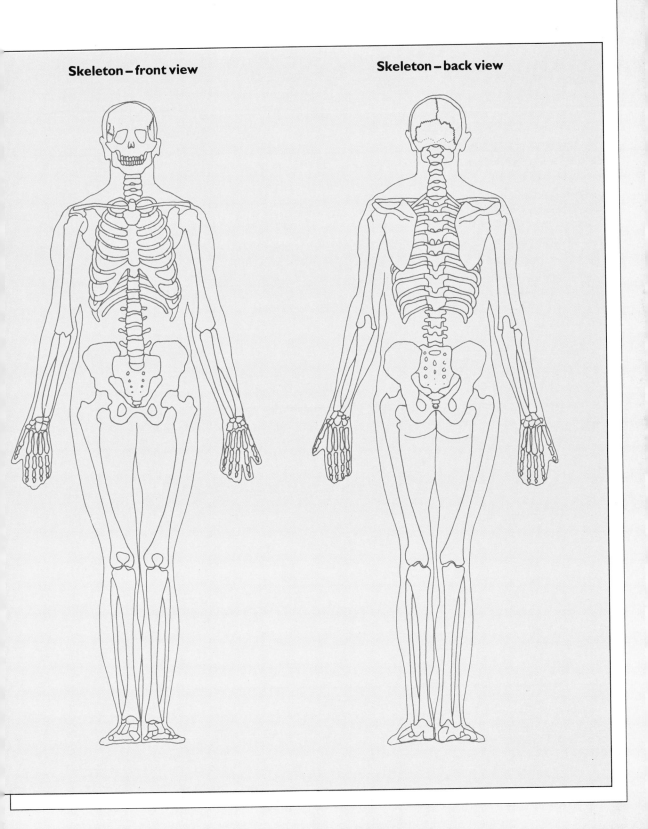

Skeleton – front view

Skeleton – back view

Joints

The joints or articulations perform two functions. They bind the bones firmly to each other by ligaments, and they permit movement between them.

The joints are at the root of all movement; without them our bodies would be rigid and immobile. Using the joints the bones, like levers, are pulled into movement, by their attached muscles. All the movements that you make with your body you direct through your skeleton.

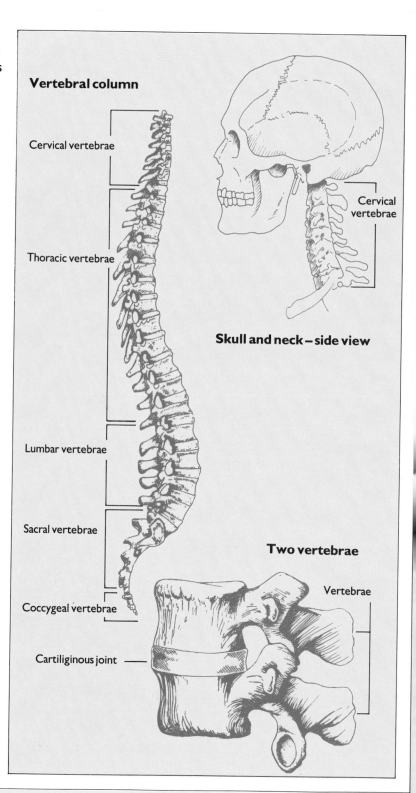

Vertebral column

Cervical vertebrae

Thoracic vertebrae

Lumbar vertebrae

Sacral vertebrae

Coccygeal vertebrae

Cartiliginous joint

Cervical vertebrae

Skull and neck – side view

Two vertebrae

Vertebrae

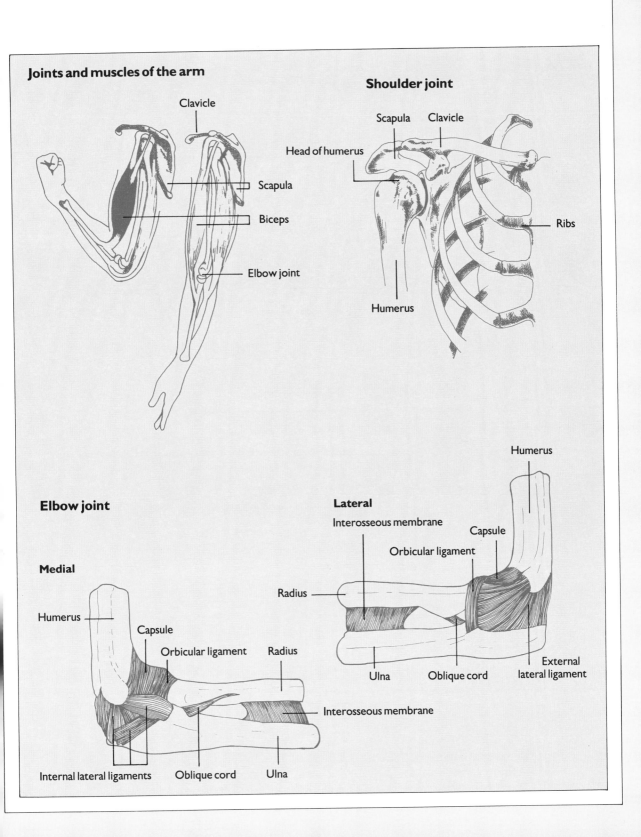

Joints and muscles of the arm

Clavicle

Scapula

Biceps

Elbow joint

Shoulder joint

Scapula Clavicle

Head of humerus

Ribs

Humerus

Elbow joint

Medial

Humerus

Capsule

Orbicular ligament Radius

Internal lateral ligaments Oblique cord Ulna

Lateral

Interosseous membrane

Orbicular ligament

Capsule

Radius

Humerus

Ulna Oblique cord

External
lateral ligament

Interosseous membrane

Hip joint

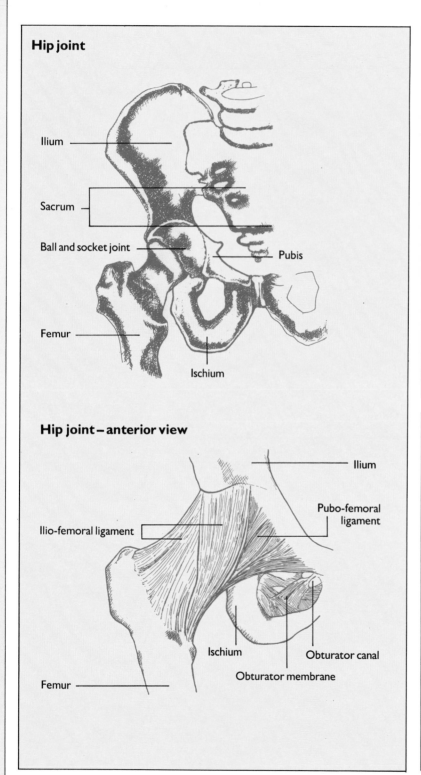

Ilium

Sacrum

Ball and socket joint

Pubis

Femur

Ischium

Hip joint – anterior view

Ilium

Pubo-femoral ligament

Ilio-femoral ligament

Ischium

Obturator canal

Obturator membrane

Femur

Knee joint

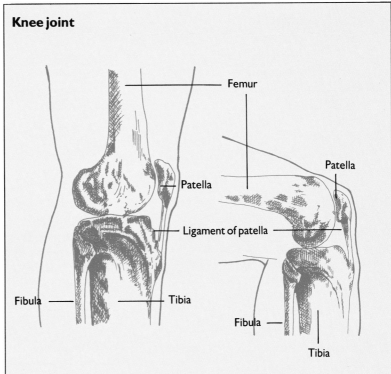

Femur

Patella

Patella

Ligament of patella

Fibula   Tibia

Fibula

Tibia

Ankle joint – outer side

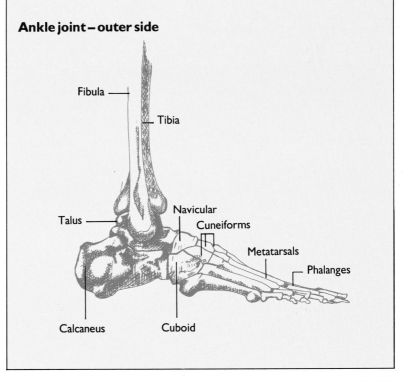

Fibula

Tibia

Navicular

Cuneiforms

Talus

Metatarsals

Phalanges

Calcaneus   Cuboid

Muscles

Not only do the muscles provide your body with its contours. More importantly, they are attached to the bones and are responsible for moving them. When you lift your arm or your leg, for example, many muscles become involved, all acting together to comply with the way in which you direct your bones.

The muscles are organs of energy and potential power and their ability to be active and passive are the two essential ingredients of all movement. In movement the muscles work as mutual opposites; as one muscle becomes active, contracts and shortens to pull the bone into motion, so its partner becomes passive, relaxes and stretches to allow the bone to be moved from its joint.

Your muscles are also major organs of sensation, contracting and relaxing in response to pleasure and pain and to changes in the temperature of your environment.

Your muscles protect your body and in response to a fall or a blow they will contract in order to minimise pain and contain the injury. Your muscles will also contract in response to an emotional threat or upheaval, especially in those areas of the body that are not protected by the bones, such as the neck, throat and abdomen.

The importance of exercise

The main function of the musculo-skeletal system is to position and move your body through space. If the potential of this system is not used regularly it will decline; this is why some form of exercise should be used to maintain and improve its performance. Such exercise should be directed towards an even development of the body and should therefore include both static exercise for relaxation and flexibility, and dynamic exercise for strength and endurance.

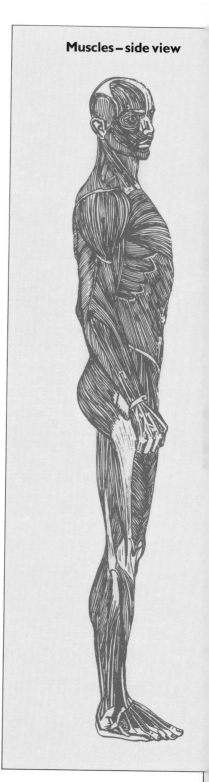

Muscles – side view

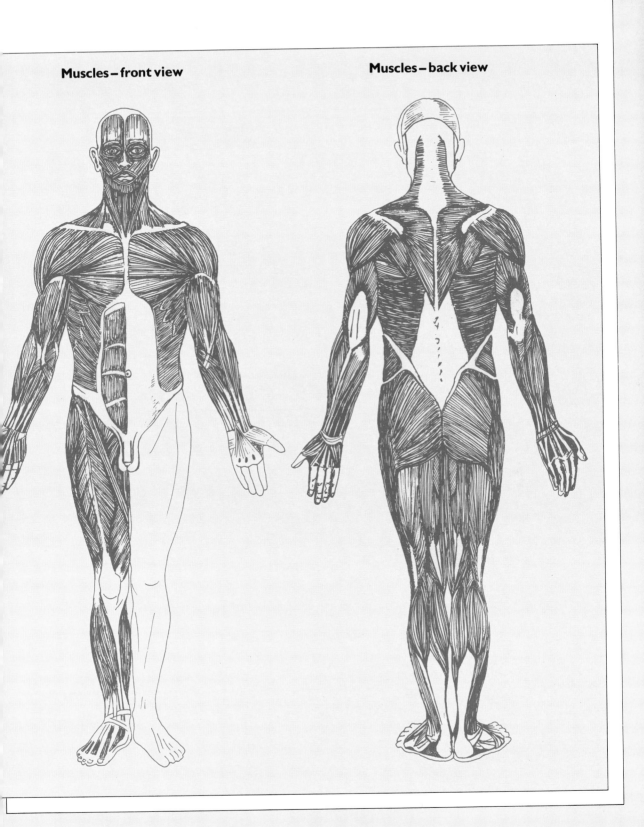

Muscles – front view

Muscles – back view

Respiratory system

Life depends upon movement, movement depends upon energy and energy depends upon oxygen. The body can exist for weeks without food, days without water, but only minutes without the oxygen supplied through respiration. Oxygen is a vital ingredient for the conversion of nutrients to energy – a process known as oxidation. Respiration also removes carbon dioxide, the waste product of oxidation. Oxygen supply, carbon dioxide elimination and breath control are thus the basic activities of respiration.

The respiratory system includes the nose and mouth, the airways leading to the lungs – the pharynx, trachea and bronchi – and the lung and chest structures responsible for the movement of air. The main airway from the pharynx branches into two bronchi, one of which enters each lung. Within the lungs the bronchi branch many more times, the tubes becoming progressively narrower and more prolific, eventually ending in tiny sacs called alveoli. The alveoli are the sites of gaseous exchange; it is here that oxygen is supplied to and carbon dioxide eliminated from the bloodstream.

Breathing

The lungs themselves are like two passive elastic containers. During inspiration the diaphragm contracts downwards and the intercostal muscles between the ribs contract to open the rib cage upwards and outwards. The subsequent vacuum within the rib cage then draws air into the lungs. Expiration is completely passive; when the muscular effort of inspiration ceases, expiration takes place spontaneously as the stretched tissues recoil to their normal length.

The major muscles associated with respiration are mainly at the sides and back of the body. Maintaining the strength of your back is therefore a great aid to the function of respiration.

Good posture

Sit up straight and draw your shoulder blades together. Immediately your body takes on a different feel and a different appearance. This kind of posture allows your shoulders to open and your chest to expand more easily and to a greater degree. Your abdominal muscles are no longer compressed and your diaphragm can descend more deeply with each inspiration.

Maximum efficiency

Our oxygen intake very much depends on our normal physical activities or lack of them. For example, prolonged rest can decrease our normal intake of oxygen by about 25 per cent, whereas habitual physical exercise can increase it by the same amount. However, during very strenuous activity the ability of the circulatory system to

The respiratory system and the heart

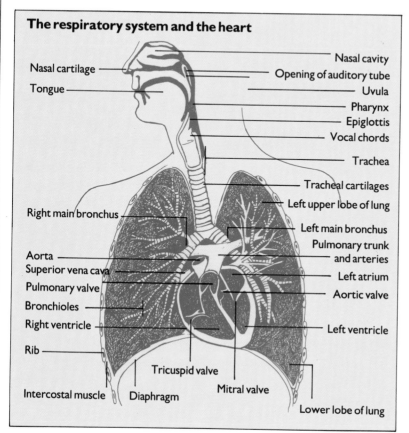

Nasal cartilage

Tongue

Nasal cavity

Opening of auditory tube

Uvula

Pharynx

Epiglottis

Vocal chords

Trachea

Tracheal cartilages

Left upper lobe of lung

Right main bronchus

Left main bronchus

Pulmonary trunk and arteries

Aorta

Superior vena cava

Pulmonary valve

Bronchioles

Right ventricle

Rib

Left atrium

Aortic valve

Left ventricle

Intercostal muscle

Diaphragm

Tricuspid valve

Mitral valve

Lower lobe of lung

supply oxygen to the muscles reaches a maximum and beyond this an oxygen debt builds up. This is why breathing often remains deep and rapid after strenuous exercise or activity has ceased.

Upper-chest breathing is shallow and rapid and drastically reduces the volume of inhalation and the volume of oxygen supplied to the lungs. Abdominal breathing, where the chest and belly expand and contract together, is the most efficient means of respiration as it allows the body to consume the maximum amount of air with the least amount of effort. Most athletes, well trained in this kind of respiration, perform moderate exercise with no increase in their breathing is rate.

more, increasing the volume of your breath reduces the breathing rate by the same amount. This means that not only do the lungs function more effectively, but their workload, and consequently their wear and tear, can be reduced by as much as 25 per cent.

Benefits of abdominal breathing

With every inhalation the carbon dioxide already in the airways and nostrils from the previous exhalation is drawn back into the lungs. This toxic gas represents about a third of every normal breath — more if breathing is rapid and shallow. Deep abdominal breathing reduces this fraction and increases the volume of the inhalation, and consequently the oxygen supply, and relieves the body of a greater quantity of waste carbon dioxide.

However, as well as drastically improving the life and energy of your body, abdominal breathing also has many other advantages. For example, deep inspiration soothes the digestive organs and promotes feelings of ease within the abdomen, helping to reduce nervous tension and facilitate a better digestive rhythm. Further-

Heart and circulation

Through the circulation of blood all tissues in the body are supplied with oxygen and nutrients and cleansed of their waste.

The blood

The quantity of blood contained within the body amounts to about 8 pints (5 litres), and consists of red and white corpuscles, platelets and plasma. Red corpuscles are the oxygen carriers, absorbing and transporting oxygen to the tissues. White corpuscles ingest bacteria, protect the body from infection and help to disintegrate and liquify tissue debris. Platelets are vital to the coagulation of the blood. Plasma holds various substances in solution, including amino acids, fats, mineral salts, gases, enzymes, hormones, antibodies, antitoxins and urea. It 'leaks' out of the capillaries, bathing the tissues in nutrients and removing waste products.

The heart

Of all the muscles in the human body it is the heart that reigns supreme. Situated in the middle of the chest, just above the diaphragm, its pulse is the first spot that lives in the foetus and the last that dies in every human being.

Its rhythm is one of contraction and relaxation; when the heart beats it contracts and empties and between beats it relaxes and fills, drawing oxygenated blood from the lungs into one side and deoxygenated blood from the body into the other. When the heart contracts again it pumps the oxygenated blood into the body and the deoxygenated blood into the lungs.

The circulatory system

Oxygenated blood circulates throughout the body in the arteries and capillaries – fine blood vessels that form networks in the tissues. Here various nutrients and wastes are exchanged with the tissues, and the deoxygenated blood is then transferred to the veins and returned to the heart.

The return flow of blood to the heart depends upon muscle action and respiration. Contraction of the leg muscles during movement compresses the veins and squeezes the blood into the abdomen, where the action of the diaphragm compresses the veins further and squeezes the blood into the chest. Here the veins are compressed by action of the rib cage and the blood is consequently returned to the heart.

Both your heart and muscles receive their blood supply when they are relaxed. Consequently the greater the muscles' degree of suppleness and relaxation, the more nutrients they receive and the more they are able to cleanse themselves of their wastes. This also has a beneficial effect on their reflex actions and their ability to contract and assist your return circulation.

The aerobic process

Everyone knows what aerobic means, don't they? Or do they?

The aerobic process in fact is nothing more than the means by which oxygen is transported from your lungs to your muscles via the bloodstream. The muscles then use the oxygen to help create the energy that powers their movements. This process is constant and

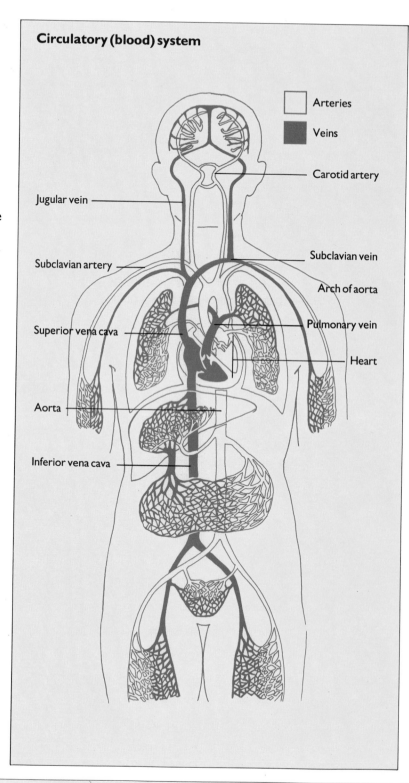

Circulatory (blood) system

Arteries

Veins

Jugular vein

Subclavian artery

Superior vena cava

Aorta

Inferior vena cava

Carotid artery

Subclavian vein

Arch of aorta

Pulmonary vein

Heart

continues to supply oxygen to your muscles – as long as you do not get out of breath, that is.

The best way to improve on this state, and thus to improve the condition of your heart and lungs, is to exercise within a regular breathing rhythm, to allow yourself to become slightly breathless, then to reduce the pace for a quick recovery. In this way your strength, endurance and ability to exercise is developed harmoniously within the limits of your body.

The anaerobic process

As long as the body's activities remain within the limits of the respiration rate, the heart keeps the muscles supplied with oxygen throughout the aerobic process. However, when the muscles perform at high intensity the aerobic process can no longer keep up with the muscles' demand for energy, and breathlessness starts. And it is at this point that the anaerobic process takes over.

During activity, energy-rich molecules are broken down in the presence of oxygen, providing the muscles with their energy. If intense activity continues and the bloodstream is unable to transport oxygen to the muscles rapidly enough, a different series of chemical reactions occur in the muscles. These reactions do not need oxygen, and they result in a build-up of lactic acid.

This is known as anaerobic activity, and it becomes apparent when the muscles start to ache and the limbs become heavy and tired. The period of rapid breathing following such activity repays this oxygen debt that has accumulated, it clears the lactic acid and it restores the muscles to a normal state.

Although anaerobic activity can improve your muscular endurance, this kind of exercise is best practised when your aerobic activity is strong, and then only for short periods with ample recovery time. Such regular exercise greatly improves the aerobic process, which in turn improves your body's ability to withstand fatigue. At the same time, the quality of the blood improves as it becomes enriched with haemoglobin in the red blood cells that transport oxygen, and it reduces the level of triglycerides, small globules of fat that are implicated in heart disorders. All in all, through the regular practice of appropriate enjoyable exercises, the function of the heart, the quality of the blood and the health of the blood vessels through which it is transported are all vastly improved.

Digestion

We must eat to live, and the food that we eat is our body's only source of energy. Without it we die.

Before food can be utilised as energy it must be liquidised, and this is effected by a variety of secretions. Once liquidised, its nutrients can then be absorbed into the bloodstream for easy transportation through the body. The digestive organs prepare your food for cellular use. They break down solid foods to a liquid form, absorb their nutrients and the liquid and excrete the remainder.

All this takes place within the alimentary canal, an open-ended tube that travels from your mouth to your anus and includes the oesophagus, stomach, small and large intestine. Food travels this canal through the action of peristalsis – the rhythmic contraction and relaxation of its muscular walls.

The salivary glands secrete from the roof of the mouth and beneath the tongue. Once chewed and mixed with saliva, food is rolled into a ball and passed down the oesophagus to the stomach. The stomach lies in the upper part of the abdomen under the diaphragm and food remains here for some three or four hours. During this time it is churned into smaller pieces, mixed with gastric juices and hydrochloric acid and lubricated with mucus, so that on leaving the stomach the food is about 80 per cent liquid, called chyme.

Once passed into the small intestine, chyme is mixed with intestinal juices and secretions from the pancreas and gall bladder. Here it remains for another four to five hours, during which time the nutrients are absorbed through the intestinal walls into the bloodstream. The remainder is called chyle and this is passed into the large intestine, where it remains for five to twenty-five hours or more. During this time salts, liquid and minerals are absorbed in the same way and the remainder is mixed with mucus and stored until defaecated.

The food you eat

Because it is vital to the health and performance of your body, you should consider what effect each meal will have upon your body, rather than what it is going to taste like. From the vast selection of foods that are available, it should not be difficult to reach a compromise and find the kinds of food that meet your body's requirements *and* satisfy your taste buds.

The importance of providing your body with proper nutrients, and eating food that will pass easily through your digestive system and not clog and putrefy in your intestines, cannot be overstressed. It is an ancient concept that the belly is a source of wisdom and contentment and that the proper relaxation of this area has a vast influence throughout the entire body. Furthermore, the regular practice of the appropriate exercises greatly assists the function of the digestive system and the relaxation of the abdomen.

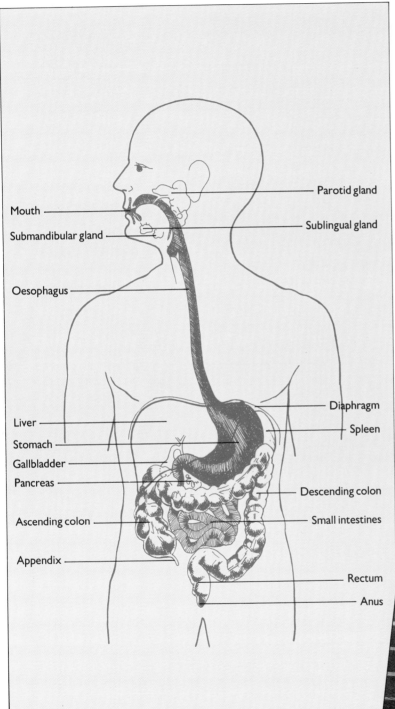

Mouth
Submandibular gland
Oesophagus
Liver
Stomach
Gallbladder
Pancreas
Ascending colon
Appendix

Parotid gland
Sublingual gland
Diaphragm
Spleen
Descending colon
Small intestines
Rectum
Anus

Exercise and digestion

Digestion is assisted by respiration, and abdominal breathing is highly beneficial and a great aid to the rhythm of digestion. Relaxing your abdominal muscles during inhalation allows the diaphragm to descend more deeply into the abdomen, compressing the abdominal contents. On expiration, as the diaphragm ascends it creates a vacuum within the abdomen that draws its contents inwards. This is equivalent to a continuous gentle massage that soothes and stimulates the gastric organs and aids their functions.

Regular exercise relieves stress and decreases the individual's susceptibility to external pressures, one of the major causes of disorders of the digestive system. Static exercise increases the abdominal circulation, while dynamic exercise improves peristalis. With proper exercise the digestive process becomes more efficient, food is more easily assimilated, and the body's waste products pass more regularly through the system.

The nervous system

For all the various parts of the body to work together as an organised whole, a general means of communication and control is vital. This is the responsibility of the nervous system. It deals with the coordination of the body's functions and activities through the rapid conduction of messages, in the form of electrical impulses, from one part of the body to another.

The central nervous system is enclosed within the spinal column and skull, or cranium, and consists of the spinal cord and the brain. The autonomic nervous system is situated in front of the spinal column and joins the central system at various intervals along the spinal column.

The brain

This is the centre of control for all physical and mental activity. It integrates conscious and unconscious activity, all movement, the senses like sight, sound, touch, taste, smell and balance, and higher functions like memory, speech, emotion, thought and intellect. Any interference with the brain can thus radically alter human behaviour. A blow on the head, for example, can affect the entire nervous system in such a way as to render the recipient totally unconscious with no movement or response to stimulation. Similarly, a severe emotional trauma can render the recipient speechless or dumb, rigid (scared stiff) or even unconscious. The brain, then, is crucial to the health and coordination of the human body and all its powers.

The spinal cord

This extends from the brain to the base of the spine. Two nerve roots project from between each of the spinal vertebrae, and these nerve roots then multiply to serve the skin, muscles and joints.

The central nervous system is responsible for all voluntary or willed movements of muscles and bones, and because of this it is also known as the voluntary nervous system.

The autonomic nervous system

From the two cords situated on each side of the front of the spine, nerve roots project to various nerve centres that are situated at intervals along the column. From these centres the autonomic nervous system serves all the body's various organs and glands, stimulating or inhibiting their functions. This part of the nervous system serves the parts of the body over which we have little or no control and because of this it is also known as the involuntary nervous system.

Integration and learning

The nervous system integrates activities, receives incoming information through its sensory nerves and responds with messages through outgoing nerves. Perhaps complete understanding of the human nervous system will always be elusive, and it has even been suggested that maybe the brain falls short of the ability to comprehend its own complexities.

It was long taken for granted, for example, that the voluntary nervous system was the only part of the nervous system connected with learning. However, fairly recent developments in human autonomic learning has shown that learning can also take place through the involuntary nervous system and visceral, or organic, responses.

Nervous disorders

Restlessness, insomnia, anxiety, lack of clarity and poor concentration are some disorders attributed to the nervous system. Being strung out, wound up, over-tense, at breaking point – these are all terms used to describe nervous conditions. Disorders like these, however, are often more to do with the musculoskeletal system than the nervous system.

Pressures of work, family life, environment, relationships and so on are some external influences that subscribe to these kinds of 'nervous' conditions, but quite often internal factors can also be responsible. Poor respiration, poor digestion, a lack of proper exercise and rest can all contribute towards undermining the stability of the nervous system and result in 'nervous' conditions.

Shallow breathing, for example, is known by physical therapists to be a cause of apathy, irritability and loss of self control. The less oxygen that reaches the tissues, the more the body becomes distressed and this condition can quite often result in a state of extreme anxiety, with no apparent reason.

A lack of proper nutrition can also cause symptoms of nervous disorders, while food that cannot

Central nervous system

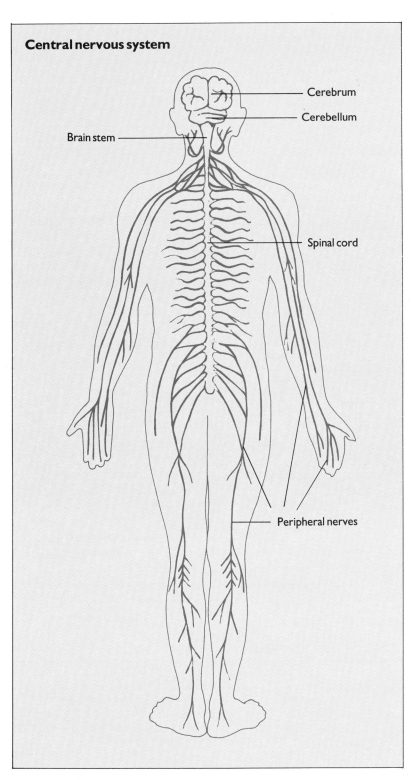

Cerebrum

Cerebellum

Brain stem

Spinal cord

Peripheral nerves

be digested easily, or compacts in the large intestine, causes restlessness, irritability, loss of clarity and concentration. Even the muscles and joints, when not properly exercised, can overload the nervous system with constant messages of aches and pains, and this can lead to a breakdown in communication whereby the affected muscles and joints lose some of their movement and sensation, becoming partially paralysed and numb.

Exercise and the nervous system

All this can be prevented and relieved with the regular use of appropriate exercise. Even your brain is influenced by such exercise and this is quite often why, after a period of intense exercise, although the muscles may be tired, the brain becomes more active. This happens with dynamic endurance exercises and inverted static exercises like headstands which increases the brain's blood sugar level – the essence of all its activity.

The nervous system is also the body's protector, emitting intense signals when something is amiss or going amiss. These sensations of pain arouse the nervous system and raise the heart rate, breathing rate and blood pressure. This places the body in a state of alert and indicates the area that needs attention. If the pain is then relieved, all well and good, but if the pain is allowed to continue, energy is wasted and stress is placed upon the essential organs. Because of this, relieving stiffness through appropriate exercises conserves energy and benefits the major systems that support your body.

The endocrine system

The endocrine glands produce secretions that regulate the body's chemistry. They produce secretions called hormones that are carried round in the bloodstream and influence target areas of the body. For example, you've probably heard of the hormone insulin; this is produced in the pancreas but it acts on the liver. The effect of most hormones is to bring about a slow and gradual change in the body, over a period of time.

Seven major glands form the endocrine system, and each contributes to the balance of the others – they all interact.

Endocrine system

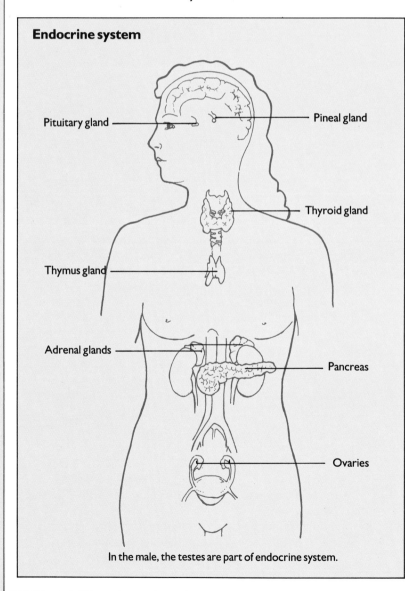

Pituitary gland

Thymus gland

Adrenal glands

Pineal gland

Thyroid gland

Pancreas

Ovaries

In the male, the testes are part of endocrine system.

Pituitary
The pituitary gland is situated in the skull, in line with the bridge of the nose. It is perhaps the most important of the endocrine glands, producing a variety of hormones that regulate other endocrine glands – rather like the conductor of an orchestra. For the sake of simplicity, however, its functions fall into one of two groups: control of growth and metabolism; and control of the sexual cycle.

Thyroid
The thyroid gland can be found in the front of the neck, near the voice box. It plays a major part in controlling the body's metabolism and strongly influences the heart rate, blood pressure, mental activity and development.

Parathyroids
The parathyroids, as their name implies, are associated with the thyroid gland, acting with it to control the calcium level in the blood and thus, indirectly, the strength of the bones.

Thymus
The thymus sits behind the breastbone and is the central organ of the lymphatic system. The thymus stores the agents that circulate through the lymphatic flow to maintain the body's immunity to disease.

Adrenals
The adrenal glands are situated on top of the kidneys. They produce a number of hormones, including adrenaline. Adrenaline acts on various organs of the body, preparing them for physical effort.

Pancreas

The pancreas is a major organ of digestion, found in the abdomen. However it also produces a very important hormone – insulin.

Insulin controls the blood sugar level. If this varies too much you can become very ill, the most well-known such illness being diabetes.

The sex glands

The ovaries and testicles produce a number of hormones that control the sexual functions of the body.

The endocrine and nervous systems

After the nervous system, the endocrine glands constitute the second great communications system of the body. The two systems work closely together, however, the central nervous system playing a crucial role in controlling hormone secretion. Conversely, hormones alter mental function and greatly influence various kinds of behaviour.

But what has this got to do with a book on exercise? Well, as these two systems function as an interrelated unit, each one naturally has an effect upon the other. For example, nervous stress and anxiety can affect the endocrine system, just as the endocrine system can affect states of mind and types of behaviour. It is therefore not unusual for psychiatrists to recommend exercise to their patients, especially as it is known that regular exercise – as little as 15 minutes a day – can reduce nervous tension considerably.

Youthfulness and age

But how can exercise and fitness affect the whole body, not just little bits of it? Well, try thinking about the physical characteristics of a young person and then of an old person. That should give you a few clues.

Youth

A true picture of health can be seen in the structure of any infant – they are the living models of youthfulness. In their pattern of development, flexibility precedes strength – every child emerges from a curled foetal position, stretches its muscles, opens its joints and then slowly strengthens its body as it sits, crawls, stands and eventually walks. The young child builds strength upon suppleness, strengthening flexible joints and supple resilient muscles.

Look at any young child that sits and stands upright. Its back is straight and strong, and its shoulders, chest and belly are open and relaxed. The young child is a true picture of physical symmetry and through its every activity it strengthens a symmetrical flexible body that assists the functions of the organs and glands that it supports.

Age

Without proper exercise the body deteriorates and this becomes more and more evident with age. Look around you – stiff backs, necks, shoulders and legs are common amongst the older generations, playing havoc with posture and generally impairing the quality of life. Stiffness in the musculo-skeletal system is now so common that it is generally accepted as being part of the ageing process and most people feel it to be inevitable. This should not necessarily be the case. What is true, however, is that most people mature and go through their lives without ever being shown how to take care of the major part of their body – their muscles, bones and joints.

Stiffness and inflexibility does not invade the body overnight. They start in childhood as the

supply of oxygen is no longer carried to the tissues and the body's vitality diminishes.

As the chest collapses further it compresses the abdomen and slows peristalsis, abdominal breathing diminishes and becomes less of an aid to digestion and the food ingested remains far longer within the digestive system. Stiffness in the leg muscles coupled with poor breathing inhibits the venous return of blood to the heart, and circulation becomes impaired.

muscles contract in response to emotional and physical trauma, and the residues of these traumas slowly accumulate with the stresses and strains of everyday life and become apparent in adulthood. It need not be like this though. If you know what to do to maintain and improve the health of your muscles and joints, your body can improve with age, not degenerate. Inflexibility is like a disease and it will not remedy itself; it invariably gets worse unless it is 'treated'.

Sooner or later as the muscles contract with stiffness they begin to pull the body's bony structure out of alignment and off balance. The effects of this upon the other systems that support the body's life is disastrous. The nervous system is bombarded with messages, the nerves themselves are often trapped within the joints and the pain of these conditions override all the other pleasurable sensations that emanate from the body. Indeed when the pain becomes too intense the nervous system cuts out and the affected parts become partially paralysed and lose heat and sensation.

As the skeleton is pulled off balance the return to an upright posture becomes increasingly difficult. The strength of the back muscles that support the spine diminishes, the shoulders round and the chest cramps, compressing the abdomen. As the trunk inclines forward great strain is placed upon the lower back and hip joints in order to maintain a semblance of uprightness. The legs then take on the load and *their* muscles and joints become stiff from the stress of supporting an imbalance of weight. As the shoulders round, the rib cage begins to collapse and breathing is impaired, a healthy

3 You Are What You Eat

Food is fuel and the quality of the food you eat affects your life. Just as impure fuel adversely affects the efficiency of a motor engine, so an inadequate diet adversely affects the growth and capability of the human body. The type of food that you eat and how you eat it affects your ability to breathe, think, work and play, and the ease with which you are able to withstand stress and resist disease. It is the variety of basic materials contained in the specific foods that we eat that provide your body with the nutrients needed to sustain its muscles, bones, organs and glands, and its mental and physical activities.

Adolescence is a time of rapid development and the increase in your appetite reflects the nutritional needs of your growing body. During this time your nutritional requirements are higher than at any other time in your life, and the eating habits that you establish now will affect your physical and mental well-being far into adulthood.

In ancient Greek and Roman medicine the condition of the gastric organs was said to be represented by our general dispositions and states of mind. Even today people are still referred to as 'liverish' or having 'gall', and to 'stop bellyaching' is a common complaint. Japanese people still refer to the abdomen as the *Onaka*, meaning the honoured middle, and many cultures throughout the world show a similar regard for the food they eat, offering a prayer, or grace, before eating. 'You are what you eat' is a phrase that reflects the need to think of the benefits of what you eat rather than the satisfaction of immature cravings.

It is difficult to think and act clearly if your mind is being constantly interrupted by abdominal sensations and your body is not receiving the nutrients it needs. A healthy diet is one which contains all the nutrients that the body needs, in the right proportions, and which encourages an easy digestive rhythm.

Minerals

These are literally minerals found in rock and earth and that are present in specific foods. They are the vital constituents of our bones and teeth, they are necessary for the utilisation and release of energy, and they help to control the composition of body fluids and cells.

Fibre

This is a mixture of indigestible materials that is not absorbed within the body. Consequently it passes through the digestive system, preventing congestion of the intestines.

Water

Water contributes to some two-thirds of your body's total weight. It is the medium in which almost every body process takes place, and the need of the body for water is second only to its need for air.

Nutrients

Proteins

Proteins form the larger part of the structure of the body's cells and hormones and the antibodies that protect us from infection. They are essential for tissue growth and repair and provide a reserve source of energy.

Carbohydrates

These provide our major source of energy, and can also be converted into body fat.

Fats

Fats maintain the healthy structure of our body's cells and also, in the form of body fat, provide a reserve form of energy.

Vitamins

Vitamins A, B, C, D, E and K, taken in the correct amounts, are vital for tissue growth and repair and for the health of your organs and glands, muscles and bones, skin, sight, nerves and blood.

Recommended foods and proportions

For optimum health and longevity you should eat foods in the following proportions:

- Whole grains — 35 per cent
- Animal foods — 25 per cent
- Fresh fruit and vegetables — 25 per cent
- Fatty spreads and oils — 10 per cent
- Highly processed foods — 5 per cent

Whole grains

These are complete seeds that contain all the elements they need to reproduce themselves. Whole grains have been the basic food of mankind for thousands of years, and in many Eastern and Third World countries they still provide the greater part of the daily diet.

Whole grains contain vitamins, minerals, fats, proteins and fibre, and should provide about a third of your daily diet. They include unrefined breakfast cereals like porridge oats and muesli, wholemeal bread, wholewheat and rye crispbreads, brown rice, wholewheat and buckwheat pasta, corn on the cob and oatmeal.

Animal foods

By animal foods we mean products of the animal kingdom, such as meat and fish, eggs and milk, which tend to form the greater part of the Western diet. They are a valuable source of protein and contain some vitamins and minerals, but are also likely to be high in fat. Because of this, too much animal produce can make you fat and increase the risk of high blood pressure and associated diseases.

Animal produce particularly rich in vitamins and minerals includes lean muscle meat (avoid the fat), liver, kidney, fish and shellfish, eggs, milk, yoghurt and cheese.

The type of animal produce that you eat can also make a difference to your health. For example, animals raised in the wild or free-range animals on farms are free of the remains of drugs and chemicals fed routinely to most farm animals.

Fruit and vegetables

These are prime sources of vitamins and minerals and are most beneficial when fresh and not overcooked. For example, a generous salad with nuts and seeds, eaten with a piece of wholemeal bread, is a balanced nutritious meal in its own right.

Fruit and vegetables contain about 90 per cent water and so can be added generously to form at least a quarter of your daily diet. These kinds of food include cooked root vegetables like onions, parsnips, potatoes and carrots, cooked leaves and seeds like peas, beans, cabbage, spinach, brussels sprouts and kale, other vegetables like mushrooms, cauliflower and courgettes, and raw vegetables like tomatoes, cucumber, lettuce, celery, cress and water cress. Of the fruit, you should eat raw fruit like apples, pears, cherries and plums, and dried fruits like raisins, figs, dates and apricots.

However, if you are vegetarian or wish to eat less animal produce, do make sure that you replace it with the proper kind of foods — ones that are high in protein and contain vitamins and minerals. These foods should form a quarter of your daily diet, and include soyabeans, green peas, broad beans, haricot beans, lentils, nuts, sesame and sunflower seeds, peanut butter and tahini.

Salad and cooking oils and fatty spreads

During the last three generations the Western world has doubled its daily diet of fat. During the same period the kinds of fats consumed have also changed, with more and more coming from animals. Only during recent years has evidence been produced to show that too much animal fat is positively unhealthy. Consequently, more vegetable and plant oils are now being used as they are much lighter than, say, butter and lard, and more conducive to good health.

Fats and oils are a concentrated source of energy and a form in which energy can be stored. Together they should contribute about one-tenth of your daily diet, including cooking oils like rapeseed, sunflower, safflower, corn and olive oil (avoid lard), salad oils like olive oil, sesame, corn oil and rapeseed (probably the lightest), and spreads like peanut butter, sesame butter, butter or, preferably, margarine rich in sunflower oil.

Highly processed foods

These should be kept to a minimum, say 5 per cent, as most

processed cakes, pies, sugary tarts, frozen puddings and the like contain additives, flavourings and high amounts of sugar and salt.

Salt, although essential to our bodies in small quantities, will make you feel tense if you eat too much of it. It can also raise your blood pressure and lead to fluid retention.

Sugar has been described as 'pure, white and deadly'. It has been stripped of all the healthy vitamins and minerals contained in the original cane or beet, and it can seem highly addictive, drawing your appetite away from other far more nourishing foods. Eaten in quantity it is a major health hazard implicated in the development of a number of serious degenerative diseases. It comes in many disguises, like tea, coffee, soft drinks, jams, cookies, ice cream, cakes and candies, and most processed and canned foods – so beware!

Fresh foods are undoubtedly more wholesome than highly processed and refined foods. For example wholewheat bread is more nutritious than white bread, fresh meat more nutritious than hot dogs and hamburgers, and freshly cooked potatoes more nutritious than instant mash.

▼ **Wholegrains are found in a variety of products and are a good source of vitamins, protein and fibre.**

Good eating habits

● Because of the length of time since the last meal the previous day and because of the lower efficiency of the muscles in the morning, it is good nutritional practice to eat breakfast before starting work. This is especially important for students as it helps to keep you alert during the morning.

● Try to avoid high-energy snacks.

● If you need to eat between meals keep to the nutritious foods.

● Try to avoid over-eating as this tends to make you feel 'dull'.

● Try not to eat large amounts of food immediately before bedtime.

Exercise and nutrition

For those who maintain a regular system of exercise or training programme, or who regularly practise sports, games and athletics, the foods you eat must be sufficient in quality and quantity to meet the energy expenditure of your body. During exercise, extra demands are placed upon the body's fuel stores and its reserves of fluids and nutrients are easily depleted.

Regular meals are especially important to your performance and these should contain plentiful amounts of the kinds of nutrients that sustain your particular activity. For example, endurance sports like running and cycling need foods rich in carbohydrate and protein that can maintain energy by keeping the blood sugar level constant. This is important for both the activity of the brain and the activity of the muscles. If the blood sugar level drops during exercise, loss of concentration and coordination results, you become prone to errors of judgment, and mental and physical fatigue develops.

In contrast, weight training demands food containing more tissue-building elements like protein and vitamins. In order to develop the muscles weight training first breaks down muscle tissue, using them as an energy store. The body then overcompensates when replacing this tissue, laying down larger amounts of muscle to meet the increasing require-ments for strength.

Useful tips

The best sources of nutrients are always natural foods. In this form other elements are also ingested in the meal, assisting the absorption and potency of the regular nut-rients. Refined foods are often digested very slowly and this can drain your body's resources.

Do not eat for about three hours before exercising. During exercise the blood supply to the stomach ceases and digestion is suspended. Any undigested food in the gut will just stagnate, and may even make you feel sick.

As protein takes longer to digest than other nutrients, any meal taken before exercise should be rich in carbohydrate and low in protein. However, make sure that this is balanced by taking in more protein in the meal eaten after your exercise.

As the muscles burn energy dur-ing activity, so the body gets hotter and sweats in order to cool itself down. If adequate fluid is unavail-able, the body overheats and its performance deteriorates. Fluid is thus especially important in the diet, and extra fluid should be taken to provide for any extra activity and to replace what is used. To do this the daily fluid intake should be increased gradually and a little fluid, like fruit juice with water, can be taken about half an hour before exercising and if possi-ble sipped during exercise.

◄ **Fresh fruit and vegetables, eaten either raw or lightly cooked, are an excellent source of vitamins, minerals and fibre.**

4 Common Complaints and Their Treatment

Ideally adolescence is a time to enjoy the benefits of a maturing body. However, common to adolescents are a number of complaints that if given prompt and proper attention can be alleviated with minimum of distress.

Obesity

Obesity comes from the Latin word *obesus* meaning 'having made oneself fat by overeating'. This does not always strictly apply in adolescence though; fatness is often due to 'puppy fat' that disappears with maturity. There are also some individuals who are prone to obesity through the misguided nutritional values of their household. True obesity is actually a form of malnutrition caused mainly by the eating of fatty, sugary, high-energy foods that are converted to body fat due to the lack of physical exercise.

The health hazards of obesity are numerous, and some of them are serious. They include poor respiration, fatigue, bronchitis, and serious heart and circulatory diseases.

Obesity has reached such proportions in the Western world that every year some one-third of its population goes on a diet. Every school has its share of overweight students and it is not uncommon to find amongst them individuals who eat merely to relieve their emotional anxiety rather than their hunger. Quite often this instigates a situation where the more obese the individual gets the more anxious they get about their appearance and the more they stuff themselves. This is often accelerated for the unhappy few by the taunts and remarks of their colleagues. Sometimes obesity can extend from adolescence to adult life – fat children tend to grow into fat adults – and in extreme cases professional advice and reassurance is well worthwhile. Obesity is a major public health problem and experts in medicine, biochemistry, nutrition, psychiatry and public health all agree that it should be dealt with in adolescence through proper exercise and nutritional advice.

Treatment
Changing to better eating habits can prevent and curb obesity. If this is coupled with a programme of consistent exercise that slowly increases the level of attainment, this will help to give a regular reduction in weight.

Acne

Acne is a skin disease common amongst teenagers and sometimes persisting into the early twenties. It is characterised by spots on the face, neck and trunk. Estimates suggest that three out of every four adolescents are affected by it and that it is more common among males. Females however can generally develop acne earlier than males because of their earlier onset of puberty.

Acne is common in adolescence because the hormonal changes that occur at this time affect the skin. It is caused by minute skin particles that detach from the lining of a hair follicle and block the follicle and adjacent sebaceous gland. This prevents natural grease from the gland being

Treatment
For the more severe forms of acne and its effects, medical advice is well worthwhile and often effective.

Frequent washing reduces the bacteria on the skin and thus the risk of infection. Sunlight also aids recovery, especially when the upper back is affected. A change to released on to the skin in the usual way, causing a small tender swelling, with what is often seen as a blackhead.

In a more severe form, the swelling breaks and becomes infected with bacteria from the skin's surface and this causes inflammation and pus. In its most severe form the inflammation extends to destroy the wall of the affected sebaceous gland and the contents of the gland then form a cyst. Where cysts are close together they can join, and in time the skin that covers them breaks to release the contents. The subsequent healing of the skin is often slow and marked by scar tissue.

Because the condition is obvious and occurs at a vulnerable time it can provoke shyness and social embarrassment. However, it usually clears up spontaneously once adulthood has been reached.

better eating habits, fresh air, exercise, relaxation and proper sleep all help to prevent and alleviate the complaint. Too much chocolate, cocoa, coffee, sugar, spicy foods, fats and nuts are all said to make the condition worse.

Anaemia

Anaemia is defined as a reduction below normal in the haemoglobin content of the blood. Haemoglobin is the iron-containing protein in the red blood cells which transports oxygen from the lungs to all tissues throughout the body; it also gives the blood its bright red appearance. Because of the rapid growth and the increase in the body's need for iron, this condition is common in adolescence, especially in females at the onset of menstruation. The symptoms of anaemia are usually paleness, tiredness, faintness and headaches, irritability and loss of appetite.

Treatment
Once the cause of the deficiency has been established, increasing the amount of iron in your diet is the usual remedy. Iron is present in meat, especially liver and kidneys, in shellfish and eggs, in whole grains, especially bran and wheatgerm, in watercress, in legumes, especially lima and soya beans, in lentils, in peanuts and tahini, and in gooseberries, apricots and dried fruit.

Fainting and giddiness

This is a transient lack of consciousness due to a momentary loss of blood to the brain. Brief losses of consciousness are common to both sexes during puberty and, although more frequent in girls, most adolescents have one or two faints.

The general cause seems to be a combination of alterations in the blood pressure and sudden changes in posture, like from sitting to standing, especially in a close environment.

Treatment
The most immediate form of treatment is to lie down in order to enable the blood to flow more readily to the brain. Recovery is accelerated if the legs and feet are raised above the head. The weakness that usually accompanies recovery disappears with rest.

Medical examination might be necessary in order to establish the cause and long-term treatment could include more fresh air, proper exercise and a change in diet to more nutritious foods.

Dental decay

Owing to the body's rapid growth and the heavy demands therefore made upon its resources, dental decay often becomes more obvious during adolescence.

Treatment
Adequate nourishment, including foods that are rich in calcium, such as nuts, seeds, milk, cheese, eggs and sardines with bones, helps to prevent decay, and you should avoid sugar, sweets and sugary drinks and foods that help to promote dental plaque. And of course regular brushing of your teeth (night and morning) and regular visits to your dentist are also most important.

Stress

'Keep your head cool and your feet warm' has been recommended by generations of physicians as an elementary rule for keeping healthy and fit, while 'hot-headedness' has always been associated with stress and ill health, irrationality and fever.

It is now widely recognised that many of our Western diseases are actually the result of the body's inability to cope with the stresses and strains of a rapid and competitive lifestyle. As you approach adulthood it is inevitable that you have to face up to these problems, and learning how to cope with them is of great value to your health.

However, as well as a great variety of stress-related diseases, there are also a large number of injuries suffered and inflicted daily as an indirect result of decisions and actions made while under stress.

Recognising stress

Stress is generally accepted as having three phases. The first phase is known as the 'alarm reaction'; this is a response by the nervous system that initiates a simultaneous series of physiological events that prepare the body for 'fight or flight'.

The second phase is known as 'resistance and adaptation'; at this stage stress is neutralised by the body as it resists and counters the

Causes and cures

Extreme physical and mental exertion, lack of sleep, harassment, isolation and social overcrowding all induce stress. In general, though, stress is caused by extremes – by either too much or too little of almost anything.

Fresh air, mild exercise and periods of rest all help to restore the body to a more balanced state. To reverse the effects of stress deep-breathing exercises, relaxation techniques like self-hypnosis and meditation, and stretching exercises, are all very good for regulating the heart rate and blood pressure, restoring abdominal breathing, regulating the digestive system, relaxing the muscles and restoring flexibility to the joints.

situation, or adapts to it.

These first two phases are quite natural and normal to our daily lives as we cope with the events that alarm or upset us, either by resisting them or adapting to them. Indeed, this kind of stress can be beneficial, arising as it does from the stimulation of new physical and intellectual challenges, romance and the excitement of other activities that spice everyday life.

The third phase of stress, however, is quite often not beneficial. This occurs when the body *fails* to neutralise the condition, whereupon a state of exhaustion then follows. This usually happens when the situation that provokes the stress is severe or persists for a period of time; it is this kind of stress that weakens the body and provokes abnormal reactions. Hatred, bigotry, anger, guilt, fear, depression and grief are some of the characteristics associated with stress and stressful personalities.

The effects of stress

Physically the 'fight or flight' response increases the heart rate and blood pressure, increases the respiration rate and constricts the airways. Breathing becomes shallow, saliva and other gastric juices are inhibited and there is a general increase in the tone (state of contraction) of the skeletal muscles, especially those of the face, throat, shoulders, abdomen and pelvic floor. In this state the body is prepared literally to fight or run away.

Persistent and severe stress, however, can lead to more permanent conditions of the heart and circulation, like chronic high blood pressure, of the lungs and respiration, like asthma, of the digestive system, like chronic constipation or diarrhoea, and of the musculo-skeletal system, like stiffness and inflexibility. And these are just a few of the physical disorders associated with stress.

5 Exercise

If you have read through the previous chapters in the book you will have discovered a little bit about the various parts of your body and how they work. But where does exercise come into it all?

From birth onwards the life force of a human being continually expresses itself through varieties of positions and movements. Internally, too, each of the body's cells divides and reproduces itself; the brain, skin, muscles, bones, organs, blood vessels, blood, nerves and fat of the body are composed of these cells, each with a life of its own and each dividing and continually replacing itself. In this way you are no longer the person you were. You may *look* the same but your eyes, nose, feet, heart, stomach, muscles and bones have all been renewed many times since birth. A breakdown in this force means that the cells no longer replace themselves, old cells accumulate and the affected part ages and wastes away.

Although health and fitness are terms used to describe the condition of the body as a whole, health generally relates to how you feel and the condition of the body's glands and organs, while fitness describes more the abilities of the musculoskeletal system and the quality of physical performance. Health and fitness however are interdependent; the fitness of the musculoskeletal system depends upon the health of the respiratory, circulatory, digestive and nervous systems, and similarly the health of these systems is influenced by the fitness of the musculoskeletal system.

If health and fitness is to be restored, maintained or improved, body activity must be maintained. Movement improves movement and a proper system and period of time given to an enjoyable exercise routine will maintain and improve the health and fitness of your body. There are many different approaches to exercise – sports, games, martial arts, dance, aerobics, isometrics, isotonics and so on. Whatever type of exercise you enjoy, however, the fundamental needs of your body must be taken into consideration. As a basic guide for self-improvement your exercise programme should aim to increase the strength and suppleness of your muscles, the flexibility of your joints and the quality of your breathing.

Dynamic and static exercise

Adolescence is a time for development, but once growth has ceased there is no physical improvement without an increase in physical effort. A capacity for action and relaxation is vital for the movements of the bones and joints. Not only must the muscles be strong enough to move, they must also be relaxed enough to allow the movement. There is no point in having a super-strong body that is too stiff to move, any more than a flexible relaxed body that doesn't have the strength for movement.

Strength, suppleness and stamina are the prerequisites for health and fitness and, combined with a flexible skeleton, they allow us to engage in all the varieties of activity that bring pleasure to our daily lives. For those of you who do maintain a balanced programme of exercise, resistance to disease and infection, and prompt recovery if illness or injury do occur, will be much improved. The body looks well, vitality is improved and relaxation and the ability to relax while active is vastly increased.

Here we look briefly at dynamic and static exercise before looking at specific types of exercise in later chapters. Taken together, dynamic and static exercises cover all the activities and postures that improve the qualities of the musculoskeletal system and the other major systems that support the life of the human body.

Static exercise

Static exercises involve the use of various postures whereby the relaxed weight of one part of the body stretches the soft tissues of another part.

For the body or any of its parts to be moved in any direction, the joints must be flexible and various muscle groups must relax to allow the movement. Static exercise gently stretches the muscle fibres and opens the body's joints, improving the muscles' ability to relax in action and the joints' ability to flex and extend.

● Static exercise is introspective and non-competitive.
● It allows you to examine and improve the suppleness of your muscles – the elastic quality that allows them to be stretched.
● It tones the muscles and restores them to the proper degree of tension suitable to a healthy condition.
● It improves the flexibility of the body's joints and in freeing the muscles and joints from stiffness and rigidity, it greatly improves the body's range of movement.

● It realigns the body's structures and improves muscular resilience – the muscles' ability to return to their natural shape. It therefore has a profound effect upon the body's shape and posture.
● It reverses the effects of aging, freeing the muscles and other soft tissues of the body from the residues of tension that have accumulated as a result of past physical and emotional traumas.
● By restoring the integrity of the muscles and joints and increasing their ability to function pleasurably through a wide range of movement, static exercise calms the nervous system.
● Static exercise improves circulation, both to the muscles – blood can flow more easily within a relaxed muscle – and from the muscles to the heart by developing the effectiveness of the muscles as pumps for returning the blood to the heart.
● Static exercise improves respiration, increasing the volume of air intake and reducing the breathing rate and consequently

the wear and tear on the lungs.
● Static exercise improves digestion by relaxing and developing the movements of the diaphragm and the abdominal and pelvic floor muscles.
● Static exercise tends to make the body feel lighter, more buoyant and adapt more easily to environmental change.
● Static exercise is a vital prerequisite for dynamic exercise. Anyone who performs strenuous activities with stiff muscles and joints speeds up the wear and tear on their body.

When we wake from a good night's rest we stretch our arms and legs spontaneously to relieve them of stiffness. This is a perfect example of static exercise.

Dynamic exercise

Dynamic exercises are active and outgoing and often competitive. They include all forms of activities that demand a degree of exertion, like sports, games, dance, gymnastics, martial arts, aerobics, isotonics and isometrics.

Different kinds of dynamic exercise produce quite different chemical changes in the muscles, and can even produce a 'one-sided development' by encouraging the strenuous activity of specific groups of muscles, consequently developing only part of the body. From this point of view, dynamic exercises that engage the whole body equally and improve endurance are the most beneficial for all round health and fitness.

● Dynamic exercise improves the body's ability to remain active, it increases oxygen-debt tolerance (see page 25), and lowers the body's metabolic rate, thereby conserving energy resources. Fatigue can be withstood for far longer periods and the body has a greater amount of energy to devote to leisure after a normal day's activity.

● In terms of energy input and output, the average human body is considered to be between 16 and 27 per cent efficient. Dynamic exercise can more than double this efficiency rating.

● Dynamic exercise increases the strength of the active muscles and joints and the strength and endurance of the heart.

● Dynamic exercise speeds up the delivery both of oxygen and nutrients to the muscles and the venous return to the heart.

● During dynamic exercise the output of the heart can increase from a resting value of 5 litres of blood a minute to the maximum of 35 litres a minute obtained by trained athletes. With the increase in output per beat the heart rate lessens and this reduced number of beats saves the wear and tear on the heart.

● Dynamic exercise strengthens respiration, it improves the efficiency of the oxygen and carbon dioxide exchange in the lungs and increases the number of red blood cells that carry the oxygen in the blood.

● Dynamic exercise stimulates the appetite and the digestive system.

● Dynamic exercise improves the removal of the body's wastes via the digestive system, via bodily secretions and via the increase in respiration.

● Dynamic exercise improves our responses and, as the nervous and musculoskeletal systems become more coordinated, so mental and perceptual alertness is sharpened, nervous tension is released and emotional illness is averted.

6 Relaxation and Breathing

Relaxation

Relaxation is the sense of relief that you feel when you let go, when you release the muscles from any unnecessary tension. This sense of relaxation assists the body to conserve its energies and expend the minimum of effort necessary to adopt any posture or movement.

Relaxation is associated with physical ease and well-being. It has a highly beneficial effect upon the nervous system, releasing it from undue stress and developing a feeling of mental tranquillity. Individuals who maintain this sense of relaxation exude confidence, ease of movement and general physical well-being, and improve their ability to focus an unhampered mind.

The opposite of a relaxed state is one of tension, associated with anxious, fearful, bigoted and angry personalities, with mental preoccupation and stress, and a host of physiological strains that can give rise to serious physical and mental disorders and diseases.

Maintaining and improving your sense of relaxation will help you to increase and harness the power of your body. Not only does relaxation ease the movement of your body in a mechanical sense, allowing freer movement of the bones. The period of relaxation before activity also allows your muscles to be nourished with their vital ingredients for energy.

To maintain and improve your state of relaxation the regular practice of the following simple technique should be of great help. It will keep you aware of the state of your muscles by improving your ability to recognise when they are relaxed and when they are contracted. With regular practice of this technique you will vastly improve your ability to retain a positive sense of relaxation in action, and deepen your body's sense of relaxation when it is resting.

Relaxation technique

Make sure your room is warm and airy and that you have 15 minutes of uninterrupted time.

● Lie on your back with your knees raised, push from the back of your head, feet and elbows and lift your shoulders and pelvis from the floor.

● Pull your shoulder blades together and your shoulders downwards.

● Slowly unroll your spine so that you straighten its curves and you can feel each vertebrae where it touches the floor. Straighten your legs and let your feet open, and relax your arms, palms upwards, at the sides of your body.

● Without moving your body, clench your fists and press your elbows into the floor, contracting the muscles of your arms and shoulders. Hold for a few seconds, then relax; repeat and relax.

● Tighten your buttocks and leg muscles and curl your toes. Hold for a few seconds, then relax; repeat and relax.

● Now let gravity centre you.

● Feel the weight of your head against the floor. Relax your eyes, mouth and jaw.

● Feel the weight of your shoulders, arms and hands against the floor. Relax your shoulders.

● Feel the weight of your upper back and chest. Feel the base of your spine, the weight of your pelvis and lower back. Relax your abdomen.

● Feel the weight of your legs and feet. Relax your face, shoulders and belly. Wherever your body is in touch with the floor, relax and let gravity centre you.

● Now feel the warmth of your body. Feel the warmth of your toes, the warmth in the arches of your feet and the warmth of your heels and ankles. Feel the weight and warmth of your feet. Feel the warmth of your lower legs, the warmth of your knees, the warmth of your thighs. Relax and feel the weight and warmth of your legs and feet. Feel the warmth of your genitals, the warmth of your belly, the warmth of your lower back. Relax and feel the weight and warmth of your body from your waist down.

● Feel the warmth of your back, the warmth of your chest, the warmth of your shoulders, arms, hands and fingers. Relax your shoulders and belly and feel the weight and warmth of your body from your shoulders down.

● Feel the warmth of your neck and throat, the warmth of your jaw, your lips, your mouth. Feel the warmth of your cheeks, ears, nostrils, and the warmth of your eyes.

● Feel the warmth of your brow, and the warmth at the crown of your head.

● Relax your face, shoulders and belly and feel the weight and warmth of your body from the crown of your head to the tips of your fingers and toes.

Breathing and relaxation

A correct breathing rhythm is vital to your body's ability to withstand stress and maintain relaxation and to your own general health, fitness and sense of well-being. Look at any healthy newborn child and you will see that its lower chest and belly work in harmony, expanding together on the inhalation and contracting together on the exhalation. This breathing rhythm is even and descends deeply into the abdomen. In contrast, someone who is dying often breathes rapidly with the upper chest, the breathing getting more rapid as it gets more shallow.

For good health the belly should be relaxed on the inhalation, allowing the diaphragm to descend deeply into the abdomen. This increases the volume of air taken into and expelled from the lungs and soothes the belly by gently compressing and releasing its contents. Abdominal breathing therefore reduces the breathing rate and consequently the effort and wear and tear on the lungs. What is more, a healthy resting adult takes about 10 breaths a minute. If he is breathing abdominally he creates an internal massage for the belly about 15,000 times every 24 hours.

Breathing technique

The quickest and the easiest way of establishing an abdominal breathing pattern is to practise the relaxation technique described above and then, while relaxed, focus your attention on the area around your navel – try to feel it from within.

Now gently draw your abdomen in with each exhalation, as though you were softly pushing the air out of your belly.

Relax your abdomen with every inhalation. In this way you will soon establish harmony between your chest and belly and they will expand and contract together.

Try to use this technique for at least five minutes at the end of every relaxation session. Alternatively, the technique can also be practised while sitting or standing, in order to relieve moments of acute anxiety.

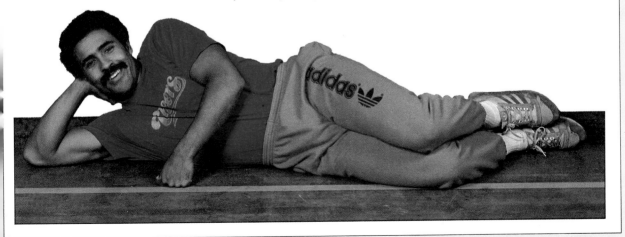

7 Static Exercise Programme

The following exercise routine is a relatively easy yet effective way to bring suppleness and flexibility to any or all of your body's major muscles and joints. If you are particularly stiff in any particular area you will soon become aware of it. Given time to deal with this inflexibility, the exercises will soon restore ease of movement to the joint or joints and strengthen your body's symmetry.

The fitness of your body's joints can be rated according to their degree of flexibility. If underlying stiffness restricts their range of movement, then the functioning of your muscles and joints is inhibited and as such they are not fit and healthy. They can only function within a limited range of movement, and if left untreated they distort the body's framework and symmetry as their condition becomes more permanent and more chronic with age and self-neglect. Given time this slow degeneration will have a devastating effect upon your health and daily activities.

Two of life's greatest gifts are sensation and movement – both found in the body's muscles and joints. Muscles and joints that contain stiffness are partially numb to sensation and partially paralysed in movement and this can severely undermine the overall health and fitness of your body.

The brief descriptions and illustrations of the exercises should help you to visualise the relative muscles and joints and, with each position, a description of where you are most likely to experience the strongest sensations has been added for your guidance and reassurance. Stretch but do not strain, use massage where shown and be consistent – practise for at least an hour or so every other day or once or twice a week.

To make the exercises as comfortable as possible most of them have been graded into a number of steps or phases. Start by practising the first step of each exercise and do not advance to the next step until you can maintain the previous one comfortably for the given period of time. Like trying to get up a ladder, you can spend a lifetime trying to jump to the top but if you are patient with yourself and persevere one step at a time you will soon get to the top.

The effects of these exercises are cumulative so, providing you practise regularly, you will improve by degrees with every session. Every discomfort that you overcome will be amply rewarded with a new sense of ease and pleasure and the ability to do a whole new range of activities.

Ankles

The ankles consist of a number of joints that are governed by the muscles of the lower legs. Together they bend, straighten and turn the feet inwards and outwards. The entire weight of the body is transferred through the ankle joints on to the sprung arches of the feet and then to the ground through the heels and toes.

Because they form the base of the body, the ankles and feet support more weight than any other part of the body. Stiffness or weakness in the ankles and arches of the feet can therefore cause problems right up through the body and can easily affect its overall structural symmetry. If you can improve the flexibility of your ankles and the suppleness of your lower leg muscles you will greatly improve your body's balance and its ability to relax while upright and active.

Exercise I

Phase I
Sit upright with your buttocks on the floor, on or between your feet with your weight supported on your buttocks and straight arms. Relax and using the proper breathing rhythm maintain this position for one to five minutes. You will feel this in your ankles and the front of your legs.

Phase 2

When you can sit between your feet with your feet turned inwards, pull your buttocks out and try to sit on the backs of your thighs in front of your buttock bones. Straighten your back and pull your shoulders downwards and your shoulder blades together. Using the proper breathing rhythm, try to maintain this position for one to five minutes.

Benefits

This is a traditional Eastern sitting position. It tones the muscles of your lower legs and strengthens the muscles of your back. It greatly improves the flexibility of your ankles and, when the posture is comfortable, it encourages a proper sitting position.

The most important point to note however is, whether you sit on the floor or on a chair, *always sit on the back of your thighs, not your buttocks*. This strengthens your lower back, relaxes your abdomen and encourages the spine to straighten and the chest to open.

Ankles and knees

The knees are the largest single joints of the body. They consist of the head of the thigh bone and the head of the shin bone, a cartilage cushion to protect them and a bony cup that prevents them from over-extending.

Of all the joints, the knee is the most complex and frequently injured. Compared to other joints the knee is relatively unprotected by surrounding muscles and consequently is prone to injury by blows or sudden stops and turns.

However, if you can improve the strength and flexibility of the knees, you will greatly improve the balance and ease of movement of your body when upright.

Exercise 2

Phase I

Sitting between your feet with your knees together, inhale deeply. On the exhalation recline backwards, resting your weight on straight arms.

Using the proper breathing rhythm try to maintain this position for one to three minutes. You will feel this in your ankles, knees, the front of your lower legs and your front thighs.

Phase 2

Tighten your buttocks to prevent lower back pain. Take a deep inhalation, push your pelvis forward and recline back on to your elbows. Try to relax and, using the proper breathing rhythm, maintain this position for one to three minutes.

Phase 3

Tighten your buttocks, take a deep inhalation, push your pelvis forward and, on the exhalation, recline with your back against the floor. If there is no pain in your lower back relax your buttocks and try to keep your knees to the floor, together or at least close together. If your lower back hurts when you relax your buttocks, open your knees.

Relax and using the proper breathing rhythm maintain this position for one to three minutes.

You will feel this throughout the front of your legs, especially your thighs and your lower abdomen. Do not tolerate back pain in this position.

Benefits

This exercise vastly improves the flexibility of your knees and ankles. It also tones the muscles of the lower belly, thighs and front legs and strengthens your lower back.

Hips

The hip joints are the central joints of your skeleton, situated a hands-span apart on the front of the lower pelvis. They are large ball-and-socket joints and, like a gear lever or a joystick, they allow movement in all directions.

It is from these joints that your body bends forward and balances upright when sitting; because of this, their flexibility is crucial to the health and integrity of your spine. If the hip joints are inflexible, the body bends forward from the spine. Similarly, when sitting, if the hip joints are inflexible, the body sits on the base of the back or buttocks and not on the backs of the legs; consequently the spine bends or rounds forward in order to maintain balance.

The flexibility of your hip joints is therefore vital to the strength of your back and in maintaining a relaxed upright posture.

Exercise 3

Phase I

Stand with your feet about 4 feet apart. Turn your toes inwards and bend your knees, lean forward and rest your hands on your lower back.

Take a deep inhalation and on the exhalation straighten your legs. You will feel this in your inside thighs.

Try to maintain the position, using the proper breathing rhythm, for one to five minutes.

Benefits

This exercise tones the inside and back thigh muscles and greatly improves the flexibility of your hip joints. It also improves circulation, especially to the head and trunk.

Phase 2

Open your legs wider, bend your knees and bring the palms of your hands to the floor, and now straighten both your legs. Take a deep inhalation and on the exhalation push your trunk back as far as you can, keeping your heels and toes firmly on the floor. Now using the proper breathing rhythm rock slowly backwards and forwards for one or two minutes. You will feel this in your inside thighs and back legs or hamstrings.

Phase 3

Maintaining the position, open your legs wider, keeping your feet turned inwards. Take a deep inhalation and on the exhalation lower your trunk on to your elbows. If you experience any difficulty in making this movement relax your hands on your lower back and gently rock up and down until the position is comfortable. You will feel this in your inside thighs and hamstrings (the back of your thighs).

Variation

If you are unable to attain this position, lie on your side with your buttocks against a wall and your knees drawn up to your chest. Roll on to your back and straighten your legs up the wall, take a deep inhalation and on the exhalation open your legs as wide as you can.

Try to keep your knees straight and, using the proper breathing rhythm, maintain this position for one to five minutes.

Exercise 4

Phase 1

Standing with your feet about 6 inches apart, bend your knees and lean forward, joining your hands together and resting them on your lower back.

Relax your neck and shoulders and take a deep inhalation. On the exhalation straighten one leg. You will feel this in the back of your thigh. Now repeat the exercise for the other leg.

Using the proper breathing rhythm, try to maintain this position, slowly straightening one leg at a time, for one to five minutes.

Phase 2

Bend both knees and take hold of your ankles. Take a deep inhalation and on the exhalation straighten both legs. Keeping your heels on the ground, lean your weight as far forward as you can and lift your buttocks.

Using the proper breathing rhythm maintain this position for one to five minutes.

Phase 3

Take a deep inhalation and on the exhalation place the palms of your hands on the floor and, keeping both legs straight, push your weight back as far as you can and lift your buttocks.

Using the proper breathing rhythm maintain this position for one to five minutes.

Benefits

This exercise greatly tones the muscles throughout the backs of your legs and improves the flexibility of your hips. Practised regularly, it relieves lower back strains.

Variation

If you experience difficulty in practising any of the phases, lie on your side with your buttocks against the wall and your knees drawn up to your chest. Place a cushion behind your head and roll on to your back. Now straighten your legs up the wall and, using the proper breathing rhythm and keeping your knees straight, extend your heels and try to maintain this position for one to five minutes.

Exercise 5

Phase I

Take a step forward, bend your front knee and place your hands on the floor.

Now semi-straighten your front leg and slide your back knee backwards to the floor.

Using the proper breathing rhythm, gently rock backwards and forwards in this position for one or two minutes. Change legs and repeat.

You will feel this through the back of your front leg, and in the front thigh of your back leg.

Phase 2

Repeat the exercise slowly until you can straighten both legs and then, using the proper breathing rhythm, maintain this position for a minute or two. Change legs and repeat.

Benefits

This exercise greatly improves the flexibility of your hips and the relaxation of the front thigh and hamstring muscles.

Exercise 6

Phase I

Sit with your lower back firmly against the wall. Open your knees and bring the soles of your feet together. Take a deep inhalation and on the exhalation gently press one knee to the floor and massage the inside thigh muscle.

Using the proper breathing rhythm, maintain this position for one or two minutes, now repeat for the other leg.

You will feel this in your hips, knees and inside thighs.

Benefits

This position tones the inside thigh and pelvic floor muscles and improves the flexibility of your hips and knees. It increases the circulation to your back and abdomen and improves the functioning of the kidneys and bladder. It also regulates menstruation and benefits the ovaries.

Phase 2

Holding your ankles push your knees open with your forearms. Using the proper breathing rhythm maintain this position for one to five minutes.

Phase 3

Keeping the same position with your knees open, take a deep inhalation and on the exhalation lean your trunk forward and rock gently further forwards until you can rest comfortably on your elbows.

Using the proper breathing rhythm maintain this position for one to five minutes, intermittently tightening and relaxing your anal and pelvic floor muscles.

Exercise 7

Phase 1

Open your feet about 2 feet and squat, resting your weight on your hands with your elbows inside your knees and your heels raised. Take a deep inhalation and on the exhalation gently push your knees open with your elbows. You will feel this in your hips, knees, ankles, inside thighs and lower legs.

Using the proper breathing rhythm maintain this position for one to five minutes.

Phase 2

Take a deep inhalation and on the exhalation push your knees open with your elbows and take your heels to the floor. Keep both feet firmly on the floor.

Using the proper breathing rhythm maintain this position for one to five minutes, intermittently tightening and relaxing your anal and pelvic floor muscles.

Benefits

This position improves the flexibility of your hips and knees and strengthens your ankles, lower legs and lower back. It tones the pelvic floor and is highly recommended for constipation.

Shoulders and Spine

The spine is the central pillar of support for the central nervous system, the heart, the lungs and the digestive organs. It consists of a flexible cushioned pillar of 33 graduated bones or vertebrae that make up four equally opposing shallow curves. The curves balance and counterbalance the weight of the head, chest and pelvis, and add to the versatility of the spine's movements.

The spine is held erect by the strength of the back muscles. When standing, the upper back muscles should always retain enough strength to keep the spine upright with the chest and shoulders open and relaxed.

The spine's joints are extremely flexible and are designed to allow twisting, side-bending, slight forward-bending and a wide range of back-bending. However, because the spine allows very little forward-bending, this movement should always come from the hips and knees. The spine exerts strength to maintain its inverted arch as the buttocks extend back and lift. This backward lifting movement lowers the front of the spinal column and maintains the strength and integrity of the lower back when bending forward.

Back bending is the true test of a healthy, flexible spine but this is only possible if the muscles of the belly, chest and shoulders are supple enough to allow the posture. Side-bending and twisting movements similarly test the suppleness of the belly.

Exercise 8

Phase I

Stand nearly an arm's length from the wall and straighten your arms above your head in line with your shoulders. Take a deep inhalation and on the exhalation push firmly from the base of your hands, arch your upper back, and rest your forehead against the wall. You will feel this through the front of your arms and trunk and should feel it in your upper back.

Using the proper breathing rhythm, maintain this position for one or two minutes.

Phase 2

Take a deep inhalation and on the exhalation push firmly from the base of your hands, lift your head and arch your upper back, taking your breast bone to the wall. Using the proper breathing rhythm, maintain this position for one or two minutes.

If you experience any sensation in your lower spine you are over-extending your lower back and under-extending your upper back. You can change this by pushing your chest forward. Do not tolerate lower back pain, especially in this position.

Phase 3

Standing with your back towards the wall tighten your buttocks and arch backwards and place the palms of your hands against the wall.

Now keeping your buttocks tensed walk away from the wall and straighten your arms. Pull your shoulder blades together and hold for three or four breaths. Do not tolerate lower back pain in this position.

Benefits

This position improves the tone of your abdominal, chest and shoulder muscles. It strengthens your wrists, arms and back and greatly increases the flexibility of your spinal column. It also opens the rib cage, increasing its flexibility and your breathing capacity. It is highly recommended for keeping your body alert and improving your strength, vitality and nervous system.

Exercise 9

Phase I

Stand with your feet 4 feet apart. Point your right foot with the heel in line with the arch of your left foot. Turn your left foot half a turn inwards. Bend your right knee and reach out with your right hand and place it on your ankle.

Take a deep inhalation and on the exhalation straighten both your legs. Rest your left hand on your left hip and, pushing from your back foot, twist your left shoulder towards the ceiling.

Using the proper breathing rhythm maintain this position for one to two minutes, then repeat the other side. You should feel this in your inside thigh and side-abdominal muscles.

Phase 2

Repeat the previous exercise, but take your hand from your hip and stretch your hand and arm upwards, trying to keep both shoulders in line with each other.

Using the proper breathing rhythm, maintain this position for one or two minutes.

Benefits

This exercise tones the inside thigh and side-abdominal muscles, improves the flexibility of your upper spine and hip joints, strengthens the ankles and opens the rib cage and shoulders. It also improves breathing capacity and is recommended for relieving backache.

Exercise 10

Lie on your back, bend your knees and, keeping both knees and feet together, rotate to the right from your hips and take your legs to the floor. Keep both feet together and hold your knees to the ground with your right hand.

Take a deep inhalation and on the exhalation extend your left arm below your shoulder line and, using the weight of your arm, rotate your shoulders and try to hold the back of both shoulders against the floor.

Using the proper breathing rhythm, maintain this position for one or two minutes, then repeat the other side. You will feel this in your buttocks and shoulders.

Benefits
This position improves the flexibility of your upper spine, it opens your chest and shoulders and tones the buttocks and side-abdominal muscles. It is also recommended for relieving backache.

Head and neck

The head is balanced on the top of the spinal column. It is due to the equal pull from the muscles on all sides of the neck that the head is kept 'elevated'. Together the muscles and joints of the neck allow the head to rotate in line with each shoulder, bend sideways so that the ear rests on the shoulder, and bend forward and backwards.

Stiff neck muscles compress the vertebrae and pull the head off balance. Their tensions are also transmitted across the top of the head and they are thus the main cause of headaches.

Exercise 11

Phase 1

Lie on your back and lift your legs and feet towards the ceiling, supporting your back with your hands. Using the proper breathing rhythm, maintain this position for one to five minutes: you will feel this in your upper spine and neck.

Phase 2
Now do splits and drop one leg backwards and the other forwards.

Now take one foot over your head to the floor and try to keep your other leg pointing towards the ceiling. Maintain this position for two or three deep breaths and repeat for the other side.

Phase 3

Take both feet over your head to the floor keeping your legs straight. Using the proper breathing rhythm, maintain this position for a minute or two. You will feel this in your neck and the backs of your legs.

Phase 4

Now bend your knees to the floor one each side of each ear and straighten your arms behind your back. Using the proper breathing rhythm, maintain this position for one to three minutes. You will feel this in your upper back and neck.

Benefits

These postures improve the flexibility of the neck. They relieve backache, strengthen the lower back, improve circulation to the spine, thyroid, parathyroid, neck and chest.

Exercise 12

Phase 1

Stand up straight, relax your shoulders and open your feet about a foot apart. Take a deep inhalation and on the exhalation lean your head and trunk to your left, keeping your chin tucked in. Try to get your left ear to touch your shoulder. You will feel this on the right side of your neck and shoulder.

Using the proper breathing rhythm, maintain this position for one to two minutes. Now repeat the other side.

Phase 2

Lift your head, straighten your back, relax your shoulders and pull your shoulder blades together. Take a deep inhalation and on the exhalation take your head as far back as you can, projecting your jaw. You will feel this in your throat.

Using the proper breathing rhythm, try to maintain this position for a minute or two.

Phase 3

Standing with your shoulders relaxed and your head still tipped back, open your mouth and jaw as wide as you possibly can. Maintain this for about half a minute.

Benefits

This exercise tones the side-neck and throat muscles, and releases tension in your face and jaw.

8 Yoga and T'ai Chi

Those of you that know a little bit about yoga will have recognised some of the static exercises in Chapter 7 as standard yoga positions. Of all the systems of static exercise, yoga is perhaps the most balanced and well-coordinated – it is certainly the oldest, with a history stretching back thousands of years.

T'ai chi is not quite as old as yoga. It consists of a mixture of static and dynamic exercises, blended together into graceful movements that look almost like a form of ballet.

The emphasis in both yoga and T'ai chi is not only on a healthy and supple body but also on inner peace and tranquillity. They both look at the person as a single unit.

Yoga

The origins of yoga are unknown but from archaeological excavations it is recognised as being at least 6,000 years old and to have been widely practised from India to Egypt. The earliest traces of yoga are those found in the ruins of ancient cities in the Indus valley, known to have seen civilisations flourishing around the year 4,000 BC. At some of these sites little figures seated in the lotus posture were found, indicating that yoga was being practised at that time.

The word yoga in fact means union and is used to describe various systems for developing physical, mental and spiritual health and uniting each individual with their true potentials. Various forms of yoga are practised, including karma yoga, raja yoga, mantra yoga, gnana yoga and bhakti yoga, but all of them have the same aim – inner peace and happiness.

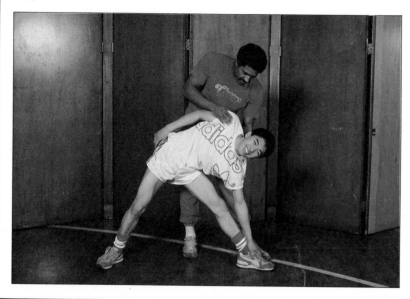

Hatha yoga

The yoga most widely practised in the Western world is hatha yoga. This consists of a collection of traditional exercises, postures and positions that lead to mastery of the body. *Ha* in fact means sun and *tha* means moon; hence hatha yoga means the joining of the sun and the moon or the development of both the masculine and feminine aspects of the human being and their union in a well-balanced and healthy individual.

The actual formulation of this system is credited to Patanjali who lived about 300 BC. He was not the creator of the techniques of hatha yoga, but he did write down descriptions of the positions and exercises that had been shown to be beneficial over centuries of experience.

Hatha yoga includes what are called the eight limbs of yoga progress – restraint, observance, postures, breath, withdrawal, concentration, meditation and illumination. Of these eight, those most practised are postures, breath and meditation.

The postures

The postures are known as asanas. They are a series of exercises that are skilfully directed towards the development of suppleness and flexibility, through stretching, and strength, developed by remaining in positions for progressive lengths of time. Certain asanas also develop balance and coordination.

Different asanas relate to specific organs and glands, increasing or reducing their blood circulation and nervous stimulation, influencing and improving their function.

The postures or asanas are practised without haste and are considered perfected when they can be performed effortlessly.

Pranayama

Breathing exercises are given great significance in hatha yoga, both for cleansing and healing and for reducing the tension of the mind and body.

You are probably well aware that your respiration fluctuates quite widely, depending on the circumstances. For example, anger and anxiety agitate the respiration, with fear it initially ceases and then becomes fast and shallow while concentration slows the respiration rate and makes it more rhythmic. Pranayama is a technique that uses this relationship but, rather than letting the state of mind influence the rhythm of respiration, uses the rhythms of respiration to influence the state of mind.

The immediate goal of pranayama is to make respiration first rhythmical and then effortless and unconscious. It is claimed by those who practise this technique that external pressures no longer disorganise their thinking and that the technique produces an inexpressible sensation of harmony.

Meditation

Mental exercises are also given great importance as an aid to concentration and understanding. These exercises are called meditations – sustained contemplation or concentration of the mind. Through the continual practice of meditation a current of unified thought arises, but this is only possible when you have sufficient control of the body (through the practice of asanas) and have learnt how to calm any mental agitation.

The unity of thought is brought about by focusing attention on a given area within the body or on a sound or an object. The given sound for meditation is known as a mantra and consists of a syllable, a word or a group of words, while a given object is known as a yantra and consists of an image of divinity, a complex design or a given diagram.

Going further

There are many different kinds of breathing and meditation techniques and there are numerous yoga institutions and foundations where they are taught and practised. Most of these foundations are named after the individuals that established them and traditionally these individuals are afforded deep reverence by those who live and work in the foundations.

The static exercise routine and the breathing and relaxation techniques present an elementary introduction to the practice of yoga. Having practised these with a reasonable degree of progression, a reputable foundation will give the guidance necessary for taking your knowledge of yoga further.

T'ai chi chuan

The history of the Eastern martial arts is obscure, as most of the ancient techniques were developed through years of dedication and passed on only by word of mouth to a worthy few. However the Shaolin monastery figures largely in this history, as many martial art forms are said to have originated from Shaolin Ch'uan-fa or Shaolin temple boxing, the martial art that evolved from the Shaolin temple in Wei, China.

Bodhidharma, an Indian Buddhist monk who resided at this monastery in the early sixth century, taught exercises, meditation and breathing techniques on which Shaolin temple boxing is thought to have been based. The teachings of Bodhidharma are also thought to form the basis of Zen meditation and he is widely regarded as the patron saint of many martial arts. Although fighting arts existed before the arrival of Bodhidharma, he instilled the idea of practising to improve health, fitness and inner harmony and his exercises and breathing techniques, probably based on yoga, caused a re-evaluation of the fighting arts and the way in which they were being practised.

Generally the martial arts are classified as hard and soft, although facets of each are included in both. Put simply, the hard martial arts meet force with force and develop a very fast series of blows as an instantaneous response to an attack, one which leads to the immediate destruction of the attacker. You may have seen examples of these lightning-quick responses in the many martial-arts movies that were popular not so long ago. In contrast, the soft arts place emphasis on the necessity for outwitting an opponent, on making use of the incoming force by side-stepping the attack and then turning the force against the attacker, and sometimes adding to it to increase the effect.

The soft arts are said to have evolved from Taoist monks, recluses who embraced Taoism, an ancient Chinese philosophy first formalised and recorded in the *Tao Te Ching* by Lao Tzu about 300 BC. T'ai Chi Ch'uan is of this origin and of all the martial arts this is said to be the most popular.

According to the teaching of Lao Tzu, 'one who excels as a warrior does not appear formidable'. In the practice of T'ai chi the evidence of the kicks, blocks, throws, pushes and strikes are concealed in a series of very slow rhythmic movements coupled with a calmness of the mind. By continually repeating these movements at a very slow speed, relaxation can be maintained while the body is fully acquainted with every sequence. If necessary these movements or sequences can then be re-enacted very quickly while maintaining a high degree of relaxation in action.

Chi

In the practice of T'ai chi the body is kept slightly rounded, and moves in circles. Emphasis is placed on low abdominal breathing, as the careful control of respiration is thought to cultivate the chi. Chi is the term given to the life force that flows through the human body along pathways known as meridians. The main purpose of cultivating the chi is to strengthen it and gain the ability to visualise its position as it flows through the body. Once this becomes possible it can be conserved and in the event of illness it can be directed to any part of the body or, in the event of an external attack, it can be released with an explosive effect.

The existence of the chi meridians and vital pressure points is significant both in T'ai chi and in various forms of ancient Chinese medicine like acupuncture and acupressure. Like T'ai chi, these systems of medicine are used to evoke the free flow of chi throughout the body and to inhibit or improve the flow of chi from vital pressure points, according to the desired effect. Knowledge of these pressure points is used as a means of improving the body's health and also, if necessary, to neutralise an assailant.

Flexibility and strength

To be adept in any form of martial art, flexibility and strength are crucial. These attributes can be developed by the use both of static exercise, and of one or more forms of dynamic exercise, like swimming, that promote all-round strength and endurance. Harmonised through the practice of a martial art like T'ai chi, health and fitness are greatly improved and the body is well equipped to deal with any internal or external disruptions.

Indian, Chinese and Japanese masters have practised these arts for generations in order to develop and protect themselves both from within and without. Because of this, the ancient martial art systems are just as closely bound to self-healing and a harmonious life as they are to self-defence.

9 Manipulation

The word manipulation means skilful use of the hands. As a method of exercise and means of treatment, manipulation has been in use for thousands of years and is now recommended by generations of people from all parts of the world. Static manipulations are performed with the assistance of a working partner who uses accurate leverage and body weight as a gentle yet effective force, restoring and improving ease and mobility to the muscles and joints.

In this chapter you will find a number of such manipulations which you and a friend can perform together. These exercises present an ideal opportunity to learn how to give and receive an effective form of elementary physical therapy that can be applied to any major part of the body. They form a basic pattern from which you can develop an individual approach based on accurate guidance, intuition and practice.

You will find that the exercises penetrate deeply into the body's muscles and joints. They can be used either to further the benefits of any exercises already used or to overcome pain and resistance to movement resulting from nervous trauma or injury.

Remember when stretching or manipulating your partner that you are there to assist, not to punish! Do not push against your partner's resistance with any extreme force; always apply only varying degrees of your relaxed bodyweight. For the best results, work as an 'assistant' and take directions from your partner, applying pressure slowly and evenly with their consent. Whether manipulating someone or being manipulated yourself, always adopt the most comfortable position, always try to remain relaxed with a proper breathing rhythm. Try to breathe in unison with your partner, applying pressure or weight as you exhale. To overcome any initial discomfort, maintain your positions for two or three breaths or for the given timing.

Through these exercises you can slowly gain an awareness of your own body and begin to move in ways that you had long forgotten, or maybe have never even experienced. However, you will only get from this programme what you put into it, and a certain amount of discomfort is to be expected at first. The proper breathing rhythm will help you to cope with this discomfort and it will gradually lessen if your sessions remain consistent. Do not allow your partner to push you too quickly or too forcefully, however, and allow enough time between your sessions for you to recover – but not so long that you lose your impetus for practice. And finally, before stretching or being stretched in order to relieve the effects of a previous injury or trauma, do please read the chapter on soft tissue injuries (Chapter 10).

Head and neck

The following exercises improve the flexibility of the neck and head, and relieve muscle tension in the neck and shoulders.

If your partner is the one to be manipulated, they should be lying on their back with their shoulder blades pulled together and their chest and shoulders opened out. Their legs and feet should be opened, they should be relaxed, with their attention focused on abdominal breathing.

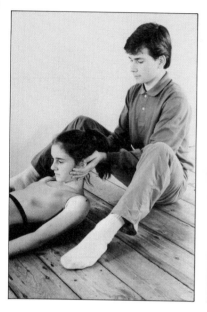
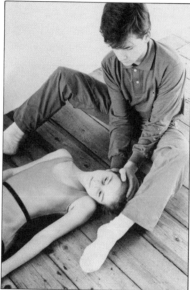

Movement 1

Sit comfortably behind your partner and spread your hands to hold both sides of the back of the head. Slowly and firmly lift and push the head forward, pushing the head towards the breastbone. Maintain the position easily by anchoring your elbows against your abdomen. Relax and breathe and hold for a minute or two.

This exercise particularly stretches and relaxes the muscles of the upper back and neck.

Movement 2

Your partner should keep their chin *slightly* tucked in and take their left ear to the left shoulder, leaving their right shoulder free to move.

Using both hands on the side of the head, push their head against the shoulder, slowly but firmly. Your partner should now relax and breathe and hold for a minute or two. Repeat for both sides.

This exercise stretches and relaxes the muscles at the sides of the neck and shoulders.

Movement 3

Your partner should now centre their head and tuck their chin in.

Place your right hand above their left ear; cross your arms and place your left hand above their right ear. Now rotate the head and when your partner indicates its limit, relax and hold the position for about half a minute or so. Repeat the exercise for the other side of the neck.

This exercise stretches and relaxes the side neck muscles that rotate the head.

Movement 4

Your partner takes their legs and feet over their head and straightens them on to the floor or, if this is uncomfortable, on to a chair.

Sit behind your partner, interlock their hands and press the elbows to the floor. Relax and hold for a minute or two.

This exercise stretches and relaxes the major muscles that lift the head and trunk upright.

Shoulders and Spine

The following exercises improve the flexibility of the spine and shoulders and relieve muscle tension in the abdomen, chest and back.

Movement 5

Your partner should now unroll slowly and lie comfortably on their back, pulling their shoulder blades together and focusing on their breathing.

Keeping your partner's back straight, slowly but firmly press their elbows to the floor, keeping them close to the sides of the head, and pulling them away from the shoulders. Relax and hold the position for a minute or two.

This exercise stretches and relaxes the upper chest and shoulder muscles.

Movement 6

Bring your partner's arms in line with their shoulders and make right angles with their forearms. Slowly but firmly press the forearms to the floor. Relax and hold the position for a minute or two.

This exercise stretches and relaxes the shoulders.

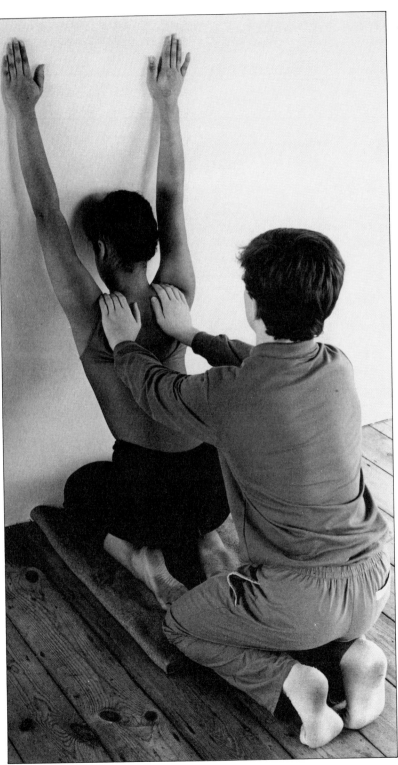

Movement 7

Your partner should sit on or between their feet with their arms in line with their shoulders, elbows straight, hands and forehead resting against a wall. They should relax and focus on their breathing.

Using your relaxed body weight, with one hand on each side of the spine, push forwards and slightly downwards. Hold for about a minute and slowly work down to the lower back, repeating the movement.

Movement 8

Your partner should be resting on their hands and knees. Keeping their upper and lower legs at right angles, they should extend their arms in line with their shoulders and rest their forehead on the floor. They should then relax and focus on their breathing.

With your hands on each side of the spine, lean your relaxed weight forward and work from the lower back to the shoulders, pushing and holding for about a minute each time.

These exercises open the chest and stretch and relax the arms, shoulders and abdominal muscles.

Movement 9

Your partner should sit back on their feet and lean forward, resting their trunk on their thighs and interlocking their hands behind their back. They should then relax and focus on their breathing.

Using your relaxed body weight, lift your partner's hands and keeping the elbows straight, slowly but firmly push them as far as possible towards or over their head. They then relax and hold the position for about half a minute.

This exercise stretches and relaxes the front of the shoulders.

Movement 10

Your partner should be lying on their back with their hands interlocked behind their head. They should lift their legs, interlock their right leg around their left and twist to their left from the waist down. They then relax and focus on their breathing.

Standing or kneeling comfortably, place your left foot on your partner's right elbow and push the elbow slowly but firmly *directly downwards* (not away from the body) to the floor. With your left hand on the back of your partner's hips and your right hand on the knee, rotate the hip, pushing the hip and knee slowly but firmly towards the floor.

Your partner now relaxes and holds the position for a minute or two. Repeat for the other side.

This exercise stretches and relaxes the front of the shoulders, lower back and side abdominal muscles.

Movement I I

The following exercise is advanced and should only be practised when all the other chest and shoulder exercises can be performed comfortably. It both strengthens and vastly improves the flexibility of the spine.

Your partner should be lying on their back with their head towards a wall. Bending their knees and tightening their buttocks and lower back muscles, they lift their pelvis and place their hands, palms down, over their head.

Standing over your partner, place your hands under your partner's arms and over the backs of their shoulders. Now lift your partner and help them to straighten their arms and form a bridge. If comfortable, slide your hands on to your partner's shoulder blades and gently pull the upper chest forwards.

Hold for as long as is comfortable.

Hips, legs and pelvic floor

The following exercises improve the flexibility of the hips, knees and
ankles and relieve muscle tension in the legs and pelvic floor.

Movement 12

Your partner should sit upright,
holding their feet, with their knees
open. They should then relax and
focus on their breathing.

Sitting comfortably, place your
feet one above the other on the
base of your partner's spine, push
firmly and hold for a minute or
two.

Movement 13

Now squatting or standing in front of your partner, hold the forearms and lean back, pulling your partner slowly forward. Hold this position for about half a minute.

Movement 14

Your partner should lie with their buttocks against the wall, their feet together and their knees open. They should relax and focus on their breathing.

Using your relaxed body weight, place your hands on your partner's knees and push them slowly and firmly downwards and outwards. Hold for a minute or two.

Movement 15

Your partner should crouch on their hands and knees, open their knees as wide as they can, lean on to their elbows and push their trunk back towards their feet. They then rest their forehead on the floor and focus on their breathing.

Place your hands on your partner's hips and push them slowly backwards and downwards towards the feet.

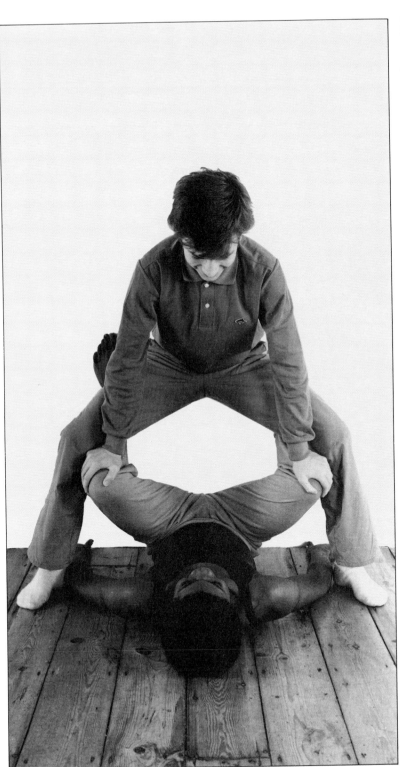

Movement 16

Your partner should lie with their buttocks against the wall, open their knees and place the soles of their feet against the wall. They should then relax and focus on their breathing.

Place your hands on your partner's knees and gently apply some of your body weight pushing them outwards. Hold for about half a minute or so.

Movement 17

Your partner should lie on their back with their buttocks firmly against a wall, then open their legs and feet as wide as they can. They should then relax and focus on their breathing.

Take one foot at a time and pull the legs slowly outwards and downwards, making sure that both legs are open equally. Now, leaning backwards, push the knees against the wall with your calfs. Hold for a minute or two.

Movement 18

Your partner should sit upright with their legs and feet open, relaxed and focused on their breathing.

Sitting comfortably, place your feet on the base of the spine and push the hips forward gently. Hold for a minute or two.

Movement 19

If these movements are comfortable, your partner should then come forward on to their elbows, and focus on their breathing.

Now using both feet, push your partner forward gently. Hold for a minute or two.

Movements 12 to 19 stretch and relax the pelvic floor and inside thigh muscles.

Movement 20

Your partner should now stand supported by you. Bend one knee and pull the foot towards the buttock, and focus on their breathing.

Supporting your partner from the chest with one hand, turn the instep of the foot towards the buttock and press the foot gently into the buttock. Hold for about a minute and repeat the other side.

Movement 21

If these exercises are comfortable, your partner should now sit between their feet, with both feet turned inwards. They should then lie back on to their elbows or, if comfortable, on to the floor, relax and focus on their breathing.

Stand over your partner and push their hips to the floor. Hold for as long as comfortable.

Movements 20 and 21 stretch and relax the front of the thighs and lower legs.

Movement 22

Your partner should stand and lean forward on to the palms of their hands. They should then focus on their breathing.

Place your front thigh firmly against your partner's upper back and push the trunk towards the legs, using your body weight. Hold for about a minute.

This exercise stretches and relaxes the calf muscles.

Movement 23

Your partner should lean forward with their arms and shoulders relaxed. They should then focus on their breathing.

You should now press downwards slowly and firmly on their hips. Hold for a minute or two.

This exercise stretches and relaxes the back thighs or hamstring muscles.

10 Popular Sports Today

Why dynamic exercise?

Ancient physicians claimed that health is present when there is 'a good bodily feeling' or when the body feels no 'dis-ease'. Inwardly this feeling is reflected in a good nature and on-going moods of optimism, while outwardly the body looks in 'good shape', that is it maintains postural symmetry and creates strong graceful movements.

Like modern-day China, some ancient cultures encouraged their people to exercise daily in the knowledge that fit people are healthy people and healthy people are happy people. The most important part of any form of recreation is to obtain pleasure from its practice – exercise need not and should not be unpleasant in order to be effective. If you enjoy your recreation you will want to engage in it more often, and consistent practice is the sure way to success.

The major principle behind dynamic forms of recreation and dynamic training programmes lies in the fact that the body does not merely adapt to the extra demands you make on it. Instead it over-compensates so that you can make even greater demands. In this way your abilities continue to exceed your periods of practice. For example, if you swim 100 metres, after recuperation you should be able to swim 110 metres, or swim 100 metres again but faster, than before. Similarly, if you can lift say 10 kg, after recuperation you should be able to lift 11 kg, and so on.

Your body, your self
It seems that no-one chooses the body that nature bestows upon them. However athletes are often fortunate in realising that they can improve upon what they have been given and learn how to exceed their limitations. This realisation can also be of great significance to your general mental outlook as it can encourage self-improvement in other aspects of your life.

Dynamic recreation or training reverses the slow physical deterioration that takes place as an effect of the ageing process. Fatigue diminishes as the body becomes stronger, and endurance, or stamina, increases. The body feels lighter, is more able to cope with specific or day-to-day demands and activities, and there is a marked improvement in skin and muscle tone, in agility and in the general feeling of self-confidence.

Benefits of dynamic exercise
This chapter illustrates the origins and physical requirements of some of our most popular sports and recreations, and indicates how best to engage in them. All of these activities vary; some improve the function and condition of only some of your muscles, while others improve the function and condition of all your muscles; some improve the function and condition of the heart and lungs, while others improve the function and condition of your nervous system.

Ideally your sport or sports should involve all your muscles and develop your body evenly, including your heart, lungs and nervous system. However self-improvement should always be gradual; realistic goals should be set for a consistent improvement of skills and potentials – you can't expect to become a superman or superwoman overnight. Furthermore, recovery time should always be sufficient to allow your body to adapt and recover from the demands of training, although it should not be so long that you lose the impetus for practice.

Always allow time to warm up before practice and warm down after practice. This lessens your chances of injury and will improve your performance and reduce stiffness, an after-effect of dynamic exercise. For the best improvements to your heart and lungs try to retain a normal or aerobic breathing rhythm for increasingly longer periods of time during your training or exercise. Check your pulse and breathing rates regularly; these should reduce as your heart and lungs strengthen.

Dynamic exercise can vastly improve the quality of your muscles, joints, heart and lungs and the length of time over which they can cope with exertion. Combined with static exercise, this fulfils your body's ability to maintain and improve strength, stamina, flexibility and relaxation.

▶ **Coe, Cram and Ovett, 1500 metres final**

Jogging, running and sprinting

Among the Ancient Greeks and Romans, running was regarded as the sport that most represented the free man. It featured in all public games and held a special place as the opening event of the Olympics. As running was considered the most noble of all the games, successful runners were held in the highest esteem and received the most favours.

In those times the distinctions between the races consisted of varying the lengths of the courses, whereas nowadays running events include cross-country, marathons, various track events and ultra-distance events. However, running is a natural activity and apart from events like these that call for specialisation, running also forms a large part of many other sports and games.

To be able to run well and sprint with speed, balance and an economy of effort enables an athlete to keep pace with others, and those that are skilful can seize an opportunity given by the saving of vital seconds to increase their lead over their opponents. Jogging to running and running to sprinting in short bursts is a natural progression that will improve general health and fitness, stimulating the digestive system, cleansing the body, sharpening the senses and improving the functioning of the heart and lungs. Running strengthens the body and improves stamina and endurance.

The mechanics of running

Mastering the mechanics of running can save time and energy. Although the adjustments needed to achieve a proper running technique may only differ slightly from your regular style, as they occur with every step, a considerable saving of effort is achieved after countless repetitions.

For economy of effort the runner's knees and feet should always point forward; any variation in this position means that the drive is not directed fully forwards and consequently some momentum is lost. The whole of the foot should also be used; the runner should land lightly on the heels then roll and push forward from the back of the foot.

The movements of the arms counterbalance the movements of the legs with an equal and opposite momentum. When running at an even pace the trunk should not lean too far forward and arms should be well flexed and kept close to the sides of the body, swinging easily to and fro across the front of the trunk. When sprinting the arms should be well flexed and raised and worked vigorously to evoke the same response from the legs.

To improve performance and aerobic activity and generally to strengthen the body, running should be practised consistently at a steady even pace that does not arouse prolonged breathlessness. Once a regular distance and speed has been comfortably established, the distance can be increased; then when the new distance has become comfortable, the previous distance should be performed at a faster pace. When both are comfortable, distance and speed can be increased again in the same way.

To improve anaerobic activity, fast running should be interspersed with slow recovery periods. And as with fixed-length running, interval running such as this must be progressive if it is to be effective; once the body can comfortably perform the number and pace of the fast intervals and fully recover during the slow ones, this programme should also be gently increased. Short intervals of very fast running, with short recoveries, can also be included, but keep your programme balanced and do not expect to increase speed *and* reduce your recovery time.

During the period leading up to a competitive event do not make the mistake of increasing your training programme. Save your extra effort for your event; just keep to the same programme and perfect your style.

A warning!

And finally, do remember that jogging, running and sprinting should *never* be performed with a stiff body. As the movements are so repetitive, they will greatly increase the wear and tear on the active joints and make them much more prone to injury. For long runs and fast runs static exercises should always be included, both to warm up and warm down, especially those exercises given for the legs, spine and shoulders.

If you practise the complete static exercise programme described in Chapter 7, it will increase your stride and improve relaxation in action. Heart and lung activity will also be more improved and your muscles will be far less susceptible to strains.

Gymnastics

The word gymnastics is derived from the ancient Greek word *gumnos* meaning naked physical exercise. According to early records this form of exercise was included, along with music and literature, in the first recorded Olympic festival staged in 776 BC.

The art of gymnastics is said to have evolved from Aesculapius, an ancient Greek who achieved such fame as a physician he was regarded as the son of Apollo, the Greek god of health. Herodikus continued the art and, after being compelled by sickness to relinquish his profession, he was surnamed 'the gymnastic' for regaining his health through diet and gymnastics.

Hippocrates was a famous Greek physician, now widely regarded as the father of modern medicine, who practised around 500 BC. He was the first to record a system of gymnastic exercises, maintaining that 'health arises from proper nourishment and exercise'. From this time on gymnastics held a recognised place in therapeutic medicine.

During the 'golden age' of ancient Greece – the time from which myths, legends and the Olympic games evolved – 'a sound mind in a sound body' was firmly embodied in the concept of education, and gymnastics was considered an equal and necessary counterpart of intellectual study.

During the period of the Roman Empire the most popular physician of ancient Rome, Galen, recorded gymnastics again, about 200 AD. He maintained that gymnasts were 'masters of exercises of youth, with an understanding of their strength and power' and that the gymnasts 'instruct athletes and others in what has medical bearing'.

Somewhat later a famous Arabian physician, Avicenna, wrote about gymnastics in the tenth century, and his writing remained a leading medical text, still in use in the universities of Lourain and Montpellier in the seventeenth century.

Later still *De Arte Gymnastica*, written in the sixteenth century by Heronymus Mercurialis, a university teacher and physician, considered the nature and effects of gymnastics and classified them into preventative for the healthy and therapeutic for the sick. During this time it was firmly established that 'the physical education of youth deeply influenced the public health of the culture'. Educationalists claimed that 'those well versed in gymnastics were far more likely to accomplish the immense achievements associated with the great exertions of the ancient Greek and early Renaissance artists'.

Modern gymnastics have evolved mainly from the work of two men, Frederick Ludwig Jahn and Per Henry Ling. Jahn's system was known as German gymnastics and came to involve the use of parallel bars, high bars and rings, ropes, ladders, running tracks, jumping ditches and vaulting bucks. By the early nineteenth century, this system was spreading rapidly and some 60 gymnasiums had been opened throughout Germany. Ling's system was known as Swedish gymnastics and was free form, practised

without apparatus. This system was perfected by Ling's son Haljmar and accepted into the educational systems of nineteenth-century Denmark and Sweden, then by Russia, Europe and America.

Of all dynamic sports and games today, there is none that demands such all-round physical fitness as gymnastics. The gymnast must be strong, extremely flexible and agile, and balance and coordination must be very highly developed. All this is achieved through proper training and the expert supervision of a professional gymnast. It is impossible to attempt gymnastics with a stiff inflexible body and all the movements that appear to flow naturally and effortlessly are the result of a dedicated training programme.

The floor exercises

The floor exercises require no apparatus, but reflect grace, agility and relaxed strength through acrobatics. Somersaults, cart-wheels, back-flips and handstands are some of the movements, synchronised with music and performed with perfect coordination and control.

Rhythmic gymnastics, like the floor exercises, also require no apparatus but are often performed with the expert use of ribbons and balls. Leaps, bounds, turns, twists and body balances are fluid and graceful, every movement harmonised with music in a skilful and graceful pattern. This is as much a dance routine as it is gymnastics and many aspiring gymnasts include ballet as part of their training programme in order to display best their flexibility and coordination with meaning and beauty.

The apparatus

When the floor exercises are transported to the beam they require the skill of a tightrope walker and the coordination, strength and flexibility of an acrobat. To work on the beam the gymnast needs perfect poise and balance; on the floor, somersaults and flips enable the gymnast to land with hands and feet apart, but not so the beam. Here the base of the body is made much smaller and any deviation from the centre of gravity by any part of the body results in imbalance.

Vaulting requires strength, speed and determination. A potentially dangerous exercise, it should never be performed by an amateur without the experienced direction of a professional coach. On the run up to the springboard every step must be equal and perfectly timed in order to hit the springboard with the maximum of efficiency and relaxation. The hands reach the horse first and these act as the centre point over which the body performs. Arms and hands then provide the power that lifts the body again, and delivers it firmly to the ground. Strength in the arms and legs for both of these take-offs, and the degree of coordination and

flexibility necessary for a hand-spring squat or straddle vault, make this an activity only for the very fit.

The gymnast who performs upon the rigid handles of the pommel horse also needs strong arms and shoulders, as well as great flexibility of the hips and legs, performing a ceaseless series of flowing rhythmic swings.

Great strength and exceptional flexibility of the shoulders is required for the rings. The handstand, straight body cross and the series of movements needed to demonstrate competence require exceptional skill, flexibility, strength and control.

The high bar upon which the gymnast performs an electrifying series of swinging circles, the asymmetric bars upon which the gymnast circles and flies, and the parallel bars all clearly demonstrate a rich diversity of skilful movement demanding great strength of the arms and shoulders and an exceptionally high degree of physical fitness.

Tumbling, sports acrobatics and trampolining are other aspects of the sport that, taken together, make gymnastics a vastly enjoyable and richly rewarding recreation.

The right combination of dynamic and static exercises strengthen the body and greatly improve flexibility; practised regularly they will maintain and improve the basic physical qualities needed for gymnastics. In conclusion it can be seen that, of all sports, gymnastics is the one most highly recommended for all-round development.

◄ **Oskana Omelianichik, Soviet gymnast**

Weight training

Weight training was highly acclaimed among the ancient Greeks, following running as the second event of the ancient Olympics. It seems that early weight training also included the throwing of weights – the forerunner to the discus and shot putt. Weight training was widely practised in order to strengthen the body and cure it of disease; indeed, testimony of its curative effects are given on an engraved stone.

· As proof of thy merit Askelepious I dedicated this stone which I lifted myself plain for all to see. Clear evidence of thy skill for before I come into thy hands and the hands of thy servants, I lay sick of a foul disease, congestion of the lungs and utter bodily weakness; but thou healer persuadest me to pick up this stone and live completely cured.

Scientific weightlifting

Milo of Crotona, an Olympic champion for 28 years, was the first scientific weightlifter. He progressed from strength to strength by regularly lifting a calf as it grew into a bull.

The basis of weight training lies in the body's natural ability to renew its tissues. Weight training breaks down muscle tissue, which then heals and builds again; the more it is broken down, the stronger the body rebuilds it, and it is this natural process that builds bulk and strength into the muscle.

Of course the body must have the right tools with which to repair itself, these being adequate rest, oxygen and nutrition. The proper intervals between training are also especially important as you must give the muscles time to repair. Training every other day or twice a week is sufficient for even development, but do not try to hasten your development by over-training or it will be counter-productive.

Weight training improves the strength and size of the muscles. This can either be done generally through a series of exercises that engage all the muscles, or locally, engaging specific muscles to even out your development. If you are a runner, for example, your legs are likely to be more developed than your arms. However, through the use of arm exercises you can even out your overall development of both arms and legs.

Before you start weight training, decide why you want to weight train. Is it to improve your overall strength and physique, as an aid to sport or to balance your development. Next, find a reputable gymnasium and discuss your approach with a qualified instructor. Depending upon your age, your muscles may still be developing and care should be taken that your training programme takes this into account. Also you should not lift weights that are too heavy for you as they will tear the muscles and leave ugly scars on the outside of the body.

Modern weight training is scientific and the type of programme you will be advised to follow will be classified according to your structure, according to whether you are tall or short, fat or thin, big-boned, and so on. It is always best to start with light weights and build up slowly, increasing the weights and repetitions as you develop, but a qualified instructor will be your best guide in this.

Weight training should be combined with static exercise to improve both the strength and suppleness of the muscles and maintain and improve your body's flexibility. If you add running or swimming to your weight-training programme, practising one or the other every day or every other day, you will have a varied and comprehensive training schedule that will vastly improve your general health and fitness and the capabilities of your body.

▶ **Daley Thompson working-out with weights**

Swimming

Swimming has always been highly popular and probably ranks as the public's favourite general recreational activity. It is one of the most effective means of dynamic physical exercise and the sense of weightlessness it brings makes it suitable for men, women and children of most ages and dispositions.

The ancient Greeks taught swimming as one of the first elements of learning and they record that from 'early years on, all capable were trained to acquire skill in this art'. They considered that learning to swim was as important as learning to read and write and a common reproach then was that 'they neither knew their letters nor how to swim'.

Nowadays the strokes most commonly practised are breast stroke, over-arm or crawl, backstroke and butterfly; of these the breast stroke and crawl are the most popular. However, whatever style is preferred, the swimmer encounters two basic forces: the resistance of the water to forward movement; and the propulsion of the body by both the arms and hands and the legs and feet.

▼ **Sarah Hardcastle, Olympic silver medallist**

Useful tips

Rather than increasing the effort put into forward propulsion of the body, a good swimmer improves the effectiveness of their style by reducing the resistance of the water. This is achieved by streamlining the body, by using the reaction of the water to the best possible advantage and by sustaining a rhythm that maintains the most constant forward momentum and that does not allow the body to sink or drag.

To gain the most power from the hands they should not be cupped but rather should be held straight with the fingers closed to present as broad a surface as possible to the water.

Because the water in front of the body is the main barrier of resistance, the head should be kept in line with the body, and the limbs held close to the sides whenever possible. In the crawl, the head should not lift but rotate from side to side on its axis with the chin tucked well in. When extending the arm, the hand should be in line with the head, and when pulled back, the elbow should lift first from the water to keep the limb close to the trunk. For economy of effort the kick should not be too high and the knees should not over bend; better to use a smaller kick that employs the whole of the leg with less extension of the knees.

In the breast stroke the mouth should be under the water until the arms separate. The arms should extend fully forward, the hands almost touching about six inches below the surface and the pull back should be outwards and downwards, with the elbows being

drawn right into the sides of the trunk. The most effective leg movement is a fast kick, known as a whip action. The heels are brought up until they are almost touching the buttocks, and the knees should not open too wide. The knees are then brought together as the feet open. As the knees extend, the legs almost touch and the feet finish the stroke with a kick.

The rhythm of the swimmer has a great influence upon endurance. A smooth even pace is much more effective than one which lifts and lowers the body or rolls it excessively from side to side. Similarly, the body should not be allowed to glide too long between strokes as you then have to overcome inertia as your forward momentum is lost.

Having a relaxed action greatly affects style and effort, so static warm-up exercises should be used for the arms, shoulders, legs and spine. These will also help to avoid

cramps. Similarly, after a particularly long or fast swim, the same static exercises for warm down should be used in order to avoid stiffness.

Benefits of swimming

Swimming stimulates the appetite and digestion, improves endurance and strengthens the back, shoulders, arms and legs. Breast stroke is effective for opening the chest and shoulders, deepening breathing, toning the abdominal muscles and strengthening the back. However, although swimming can maintain flexibility and sometimes improve it, a fair degree of flexibility, especially in the upper spine and shoulders, is fundamental for an effective style, especially for backstroke and butterfly, while the latter also requires stamina and endurance.

Combined with static exercise, swimming is a good means of improving all the attributes of health and fitness.

Cycling

The first bicycle was patented in 1818 by Baron Karl von Drais, and consisted of two wheels and a broad crossbar upon which the rider was straddled. The rider steered the machine by means of a tiller and was propelled by giant steps, pushing the machine forward from the ground. This machine was called a Draisienne and was the forerunner to the Hobby Horse, patented in London in the same year.

The first pedal bicycle was made in 1840 by a Scottish blacksmith

▼ **Greg Lemond, USA, Tour de France**

named Kirkpatrick Macmillan. It was a unique hand-made invention and copies of it were being made and improved upon until well into the 1860s. However, the bicycle that really started the cycling revolution was manufactured in France from about 1861 by the Michelin family. This bicycle had cranks and pedals fitted to the front wheel, much the same as a modern child's three-wheeler. These early bicycles were bought in their thousands and from this time on cycling became both a mode of transport and recreation.

The early French machine led to a British invention, nicknamed the Penny Farthing, with an enormous front wheel and a tiny back wheel, the large front wheel increasing the distance travelled with each turn of the pedals. In the 1870s a modified version of this machine, called the Ariel, was manufactured in Britain by Smith, Starley & Co., and by the 1880s there were some 30 cycle manufacturers in Britain and some 50,000 cycles on the roads.

Cycling today

The bicycle of today came from the Rover Safety, a machine produced by a later member of the Starley family and his friend William Sutton. With the invention of the pneumatic tyre, patented by John Dunlop in 1888, cycling became immensely popular and by the early twentieth century there were over a million cycles on the roads of Britain.

Nowadays there are any number of cycling clubs and an enormous range of bicycles, including roadsters, lightweights, medium- and heavyweights, sports bikes, unisex bikes, small wheelers and track bikes. Cycling is one of the easiest and most pleasurable ways of keeping fit; from the toddler on a tricycle to the elderly that cycle the cities' roads and country lanes, it is an immensely popular pastime and enjoyed by people of all ages. Cycling uses a fifth of the energy needed to walk, so anyone who can walk can cycle without putting their health at risk, and it can be as vigorous or as easy as you want it to be.

Useful tips

Whatever bicycle you ride it should be adjusted to suit your requirements. The saddle should be at a height that allows the leg almost to extend when at the bottom of its stroke, and it should be set so that your arms are neither cramped nor over-extended when reaching the handlebars. The handlebars should be set at about the same height or slightly lower than your saddle.

Posture is all important when cycling, so don't hunch over your handlebars with your neck cramped. Time spent in this position could be devastating and it certainly will not do much to improve your health and fitness. Try to sit back on your saddle and keep your spine straight. The occasional roll of your head will help to keep your neck relaxed. Keep your arms and shoulders relaxed with your elbows flexed. If you should encounter a pothole or a bump in the road, this position will help to absorb the shock and maintain balance. Hand positions vary and it is good to change positions and ex-

tend the fingers occasionally to prevent them from tensing up.

Try not to roll from side to side or to rock backwards and forwards when pedalling as it wastes your energy and does nothing to improve pedal power. Inexperienced bikers usually pedal too slowly in too high a gear; find a steady rate that suits you and try to maintain a smooth easy rhythm, pedalling with the ball of the foot.

Warm-up exercises for the legs, spine, neck and shoulders will improve relaxation in action, and the same exercises to warm down will prevent stiff muscles and joints after a long or strenuous ride.

Benefits of cycling

Cycling is exhilarating, it invigorates your heart and lungs and improves your endurance. Cycling generally strengthens the body, especially the legs. It improves concentration, unbends the mind and stimulates the appetite and digestion.

Combined with a complete static exercise routine and one other all-round sport like swimming, cycling is a pleasurable and effective means of maintaining and improving all-round health and fitness.

Roller skating

It seems that a Dutchman invented roller skates in the early eighteenth century. According to legend he was an enthusiastic ice skater who, bored with the lack of skating in warm weather, adapted his wooden clogs for dry-land skating.

Following this invention came skates with six wheels, three wheels and even one with five wheels that were set in a straight line to imitate ice skates. The modern skate arrived in the 1860s when a New Yorker, Mr J. L. Plympton, replaced wooden wheels with a high-performance metal variety. Shortly after this, proper wheel-bearings were produced and from here on clubs and associations were founded throughout the Western world. More recently, a new wave of enthusiasm has developed as a result of the appearance of wheels made of polyurethane, a safe durable form of plastic that cushions the rider somewhat over cracks and bumps.

▼ **World Roller Skating Games, 1985**

Useful tips

The basic position used by most skaters for standing, stopping and starting is with the feet at right angles to each other, forming the letter T, the heel of the front skate against the middle part of the back skate. This is a stable position and one in which it is easy to remain in control. From this position you can push forward from the toe-stop on your rear skate. As you start moving, shift your weight to the front skate and push from that toe-stop.

The toe push is a good way to skate uphill and this technique can be combined with strong arm movements. The knees are flexed, the body inclined forward and the arms are held away from the trunk with the hands held low. As the right foot comes forward, the right arm moves back and your left arm comes forward; then as your left foot comes forward, your left arm moves back and your right arm moves forward, and so on, your arms moving in opposition to your legs.

On flat ground the standard gliding step begins by pushing forward from the inside wheel of the back skate. The body is slightly more erect, the knees flexed and the arms held away from the trunk with the hands about hip level.

To stop, the back foot is held at right angles behind the skating foot and slowly lowered to the ground to return to the T position.

To turn the skater uses the inside or outside edge of the skates, the inside edge corresponding to the big toe and the outside edge to the small toe. When turning, the skater leans to the left or right to make an arc.

For the novice the first steps should not be hurried, with the emphasis on control. Once the basics have been mastered, speed can be developed; if you concentrate on building a firm foundation, varieties of skating techniques will follow. Don't look down at your feet, keep looking forward, with your head up and your knees slightly flexed. Move forward slowly and don't raise the pushing skate more than a few inches from the ground. To improve your stability keep your weight well forward near the ball of the supporting foot. Relaxation in action is a vital attribute for the skater. It improves your performance, allowing your body to feel and move with the momentum.

Every skater falls at some time or another, and to learn how to fall is a crucial part of skating. If you feel yourself falling, bend your knees – tuck your chin and arms into your body, lean to one side and fall on your buttocks – your body's softest and best protected part. Remaining relaxed will reduce the effect of the impact on any specific area of your body and lessen the possibility of injury.

To recover, move into a semi-kneeling position, with one knee on the floor, and place your other skate alongside your knee. Slowly raise yourself on to your skate and then bring your other foot into the T position.

As with ice skating most professional skaters advise figure skating first as a basis for learning other techniques. Other forms of roller skating include: artistic skating, using dance and figure routines; free skating, including forward and backward skating, jumps and spins; speed skating or competitive racing; and routine skating using several skating steps like arabesques and crossovers that are performed one after another without intervals.

To be an accomplished skater, static exercise is essential as it vastly improves relaxation in action, and develops the flexibility you need for the more agile skating techniques.

Before skating, warm up with static exercises for your arms, legs and spine as this will improve your performance and reduce the risk of sustaining an injury. If you wish to avoid stiff muscles and joints after a long or strenuous bout of skating, use the same exercises to warm down.

Benefits of roller skating

Roller skating has always been highly popular, especially among children, and more recently again among adults. It improves heart and lung activities, endurance, agility, balance and coordination, and generally strengthens the body, especially the legs.

Ice skating

Ice skating has a history of thousands of years. Archaeologists have discovered skates with runners made from animal bone, probably used by nomadic tribes in the New Stone Age to cross the frozen rivers and lakes of Northern Europe. It seems that bone runners were used until the introduction of iron into Scandinavia about the year 200 AD. Among the Scandinavian nobles and warriors, skating was an essential attribute and myths and legends of the twelfth century praise the skating abilities of Scandinavian gods and heroes.

Skating was revolutionised in the fourteenth century, acquiring a new element of speed and control, when a Dutchman fashioned an iron blade into the sole of a wooden clog. This led to the discovery of a simple skating technique, still in use today, known as the Dutch Roll.

In England skating is recorded from the twelfth century and in eighteenth century Scotland its popularity was demonstrated by the formation of the world's first skating club. In early twentieth-century England the style of skating was stylish and reserved, but this changed after the 1924 Winter Olympics at Chamonix when 11-year-old Sonja Henie introduced a more athletic approach, inspiring a new wave of popularity. Nowadays art and athletics are combined and modern skating is both graceful and exhilarating.

Useful tips

For the beginner, balance and control are all important and speed can only increase with proficiency. Posture plays a great part in balance. A wide stance with legs slightly bowed and the knees flexed keeps the body-weight centred; in effect the trunk leans slightly forward in this stance and the impact of the feet is cushioned with a slight bounce, the width of the legs and feet allowing the body to weave slightly with the momentum. As soon as the knees are stiffened the trunk becomes more upright, the body more rigid and balance is easily lost.

For skating, probably more than for any other sport or recreation, relaxation in action is vital. Looking ahead, with the shoulders relaxed and the arms held slightly away from the body and the hands just above the hips, greatly aids balance.

The correct positioning of the feet is crucial. For the starting position the heels should almost be touching and the feet should be turned outwards. Pushing forward from the inside edge of the blade on the back foot, you make a very small glide with the other foot. Fairly easy, isn't it? If you can maintain this for a while, you can then slowly increase the length of your stride and glide as you gain competence.

The curve is made with the inner or the outer edge of the blade, depending on which way you wish to go, and the whole of the body, including the hips and shoulders, must turn. This demands that the body-weight be kept perfectly balanced. Again it is best to start with small circles and gradually increase size with proficiency.

Knowing how to fall must rate highly among the skater's top priorities. Even the best of the professionals fall – it is an occupational hazard or all part of the fun, depending on your sense of humour. To fall without injury, relaxation in action is vital. In this way the shock of impact does not register in a specific area of the body but can pass through it. Bend your knees to reduce the height of the fall, lift your arms, and try to fall on your buttocks – your body's natural cushion. To get up, use your hands to get you into a kneeling position, then squat and then stand.

There are various styles to be practised – figure skating, free style, distance, speed, skating in pairs, and so on – but the basis of them all, and by far the best approach, is first to master figure skating and then elementary free style. Figure skating consists of a basic 41 figures, such as circles, half circles, loops, curves and others, all demanding the subtle coordinated movements of the whole body to make the figures symmetrical.

With proper guidance available at most, if not all, of the ice rinks throughout the country, the elementaries can soon be learnt and the varieties of turns, jumps, spins and spirals of free skating will follow.

If you look at any good or professional skater you will see how relaxed and how flexible they are. To attain this state a static exercise programme should be regularly practised. It's risky to skate with a stiff body and warm-up exercises should at least include those for the legs, spine and shoulders, with special emphasis on the ankles and the knees. After a long or intense session the same exercises should be used to warm down and avoid stiffness.

Benefits of ice skating

Skating maintains and improves balance, coordination, relaxation and agility. It improves heart and lung activity and generally strengthens the body. Practised together with static exercise, and combined with swimming or jogging, it provides a great programme for all-round health and fitness.

▶ **Torvill and Dean, British Olympic gold medal winners**

Skiing

Skiing has a recorded history of some 4,000 years, with rock carvings and even ancient skis having been found preserved from this period. Ancient manuscripts show Laplanders hunting on skis with bows and arrows, while more recent sixteenth-century manuscripts also refer to hunting on skis.

Skiing originally developed out of the need to travel across country that for the greater part of every year was covered with snow. Today this necessary means of transport has evolved into an exhilarating leisure activity that is being taken up by an ever-increasing number of people. Skiing must be one of the most beneficial of pastimes, and has the added benefit of being enjoyed amidst some of the most majestic scenery in the world, where the mountain air benefits respiration and the lungs and heart as much as the exercise benefits the muscles and joints.

▼ **Permin Zurbriggen, Switzerland**

Skiing today

Skiing today can be enjoyed as an easy recreational activity or a highly competitive sport. Fundamentally it is of two different kinds: cross-country skiing, known as Nordic skiing; and downhill skiing, known as Alpine skiing. Both require a degree of competence that can only be found with proper instruction, and beginners would be well advised to obtain professional advice regarding both equipment and other factors that are vital to your safety and skiing ability.

Useful tips

Skiing improves your heart and lung activities, your general strength, your agility and endurance. To ski well, or to learn to ski well, however, requires that a reasonable degree of strength, flexibility and stamina must already be established. This reduces the risk of an accident or, in the event that you do take a fall, greatly reduces the possibility of injury. It also means that you will enjoy your skiing more and suffer less from *après ski* aches and pains.

Skiing involves a balanced stance in which the ankles, knees and hips are held slightly flexed and the trunk inclined forward. The flexing of these major joints lowers the body's centre of gravity, improving balance and stability, and promotes a resilience throughout the body that allows it to cushion and absorb the impacts that pass up through the feet and ankles. Skiing demands light to extreme flexion of the ankles, knees and hips, and the spine must be able to twist and bend from side to side in order to adjust the body's weight from the

hips upwards. The shoulders must also be strong and flexible for the arms to propel the body forward and assist in maintaining its balance.

To ski well, with maximum safety and efficiency, exercises that maintain the flexibility of these joints and the strength and relaxation of their related muscles are essential. The fitness of the body for skiing is improved through practice and general experience, but warming-up exercises should always be performed prior to activity, encouraging strength and relaxation in the most active muscles and flexibility of the joints,

especially the ankles.

While maintaining this balance in motion, it must be remembered that no part of the body is moved without another part compensating. At speed this demands and improves agility and concentration and encourages a high degree of relaxation in action. Skiing with a stiff body is therefore very risky, and for those who only manage to ski once or twice a year a static exercise programme plus a regular jog and swim is essential to maintain the degree of health and fitness necessary for the enjoyment of this rewarding activity.

Football

Football was originally played in any number of different ways. Every town and village in England used to have their own team, each team playing by its own rules, usually with as many players in the team as could be found and with little or no regard for fair play. However in 1863 the English Standard Rules were formulated and adopted, bringing some order to the chaos.

Football today

Today football is one of the world's most popular and exciting games, and is looked upon as much as a social event as a sport. Almost every town has its own widely-supported team, and the game is played in virtually every school, back street and playing field throughout the country. Its popularity is epitomised by the World Cup, an event that attracts teams and supporters from all over the globe and which is enjoyed on television by over a thousand million people.

Win, lose or draw, the pleasure of playing football comes from the spirit of playing as a good team, with each player supporting one another.

Footballing skills

Football demands skill, stamina and endurance; to be able to sprint and run and maintain a good pace often decides the outcome of a game. It demands mental as well as physical agility in order to be able to outwit and out-manoeuvre your opponent – the ability to stay light on your feet and feign to the left or right when dribbling in order to retain or gain possession of the ball.

To be able to kick the ball accurately for 5 or 50 yards at the right height and speed to score or reach a team mate requires strength, flexibility and coordination, especially in the legs and lower back. Kicking and passing are the two fundamental and essential skills; when developed into such special skills as overhead or bicycle kicks and long range shots at the goal, they demand superb fitness.

Playing the ball with your head is as much of a skill as kicking; to meet the ball on the broad area of the forehead or deflect it from either side of the forehead requires strength and flexibility of the neck. When you have to jump for the ball, taking off quickly from either foot and bracing your body in the air to add power to your head movement, this requirement extends to the whole body, added to which you need great agility.

Good football demands that you feel the ball and measure its speed, whether you need to check it with your chest or belly or guide it with a twist of your body. Furthermore, to trap the ball and control it quickly saves precious seconds that may allow you to set up an accurate shot or pass. This demands flexibility and agility in your ankles and feet so that you can secure it with the inside, outside or sole of the foot.

Whether you play attacker, midfield or defender, all players must learn these same skills, the only exception being the goalkeeper, who concentrates solely on handling. The goalkeeper especially needs to be agile and flexible; to be able to catch the ball from a standing position or to dive to the

other side of the net, the body must stretch. To pluck the ball out of the air or dive without injury, a wide range of movement and a high degree of relaxation in action is vital.

Warming up

Because of the impacts and demands made on the muscles of the legs, footballers are particularly prone to knee injuries and stiffness in the calves, thighs, buttocks, hips, knees and ankles — you only need to watch first-class football matches on TV or read the sports pages of the newspapers to realise this. It is therefore vitally important that static exercises are practised before and after a game, to warm up and warm down, to maintain muscular relaxation in action and to ensure maximum flexibility of the relative joints.

Static exercises should also be included for the back and neck, and a complete routine should be included in any regular training programme for would-be professionals. For those who are not so dedicated, static exercises and other activities such as swimming and jogging will ensure a degree of fitness that will both allow you to enjoy and to benefit from football.

Benefits

Football improves your stamina and increases the activity of your heart and lungs. More specifically, it builds up muscle strength and endurance, especially in the legs and feet.

▶ **Diego Maradona, Argentina**

Tennis

The earliest records of tennis are mediaeval woodcuts depicting a French indoor game played by hand, called *Jen de Paume*. In 1874 Major Walter Wingfield devised and patented an outdoor court and this was to become the beginning of lawn tennis as it is known today. Although some significant changes were made in 1888, the basis of toay's game was formulated by Henry Jones in 1887 for the All England Croquet and Lawn Tennis Club.

Nowadays court surfaces vary, but the general rules, scoring and playing procedures remain the same throughout the world. Tennis is a great family game enjoyed by the young and the old alike. It is also an international, highly-competitive sport and one of the leaders in terms of entertainment. It is a game of skill, requiring physical fitness and concentration, balance, good footwork and racket control.

▼ **Boris Becker, Wimbledon 1985**

Useful tips

A balanced stance is vital; it precedes every effective stroke and maintains an economy of effort. Balance means control of the body's weight so that it can be used in the most effective way. The champions of tennis use their body-weight to create power and speed when driving or returning shots. This means the knees are kept flexed, with the body pitched on to the balls of the feet, ready to spring into action and able to rotate to the left or the right, to sprint and to run sideways and backwards. A balanced stance is essential if you are not to be overwhelmed by your opponent's forceful shots or

services, if you are to get your body-weight behind your shots and keep the ball in contact with your racket until the last possible moment.

Good footwork for attacking, for advancing, for playing the net and for returning to the best court position after every stroke is essential, while forehand and backhand strokes and the snap of the wrist that often precedes a successful shot means that the hands and wrists must be both strong and flexible.

The most important stroke in tennis is the service. To achieve the maximum effect the whole body must lift and the arm stretch straight to contact the ball at the highest point, while the wrist must be ready to snap forward.

Warming up

A strenuous game of tennis burns some 100 calories every 10 minutes. Not only does it strengthen and quicken respiration and circulation and demand endurance, strength and flexibility, but the body must also be able to stretch, bend, twist, jump and sprint. Because of this, warm-up exercises should always be practised prior to play in order to relax and prepare the body, while after the game warm-down exercises will help prevent stiffness in the muscles and joints.

It would obviously be unwise to engage in this kind of exercise with a stiff body, as it will increase the tension and stiffness in the active muscles and increase the wear and tear on their related joints. The body must also be fit and prepared for fast reactions, otherwise strains

and sprains are likely. Warming up and down with static exercises for the legs, spine and shoulders will help to keep the muscles supple and their joints flexible, while the regular practice of the whole programme will be a great aid to your agility, coordination and relaxation in action.

Mental training

For those who take the sport more seriously, mental training techniques should also be practised as these will make your play that bit more controlled. The consistent use of relaxation techniques will greatly improve your ability to relax when in action and to concentrate. Furthermore, if you have a particular aspect of play that you are trying to perfect, try visualising the movements before practising the relaxation technique. Repeat it once or twice and you will probably find that you are far better able to concentrate on this feature of your game when you come to practise it.

Squash

Squash is thought to have originated at Harrow School, although the first recorded squash court was in Oxford in 1883. In the 1920s standard court measurements were agreed and the first men's and women's British Championships held. However it was not until the 1960s that squash became truly popular, with millions of people playing it throughout the country.

The need for fitness

Squash is an extremely energetic game demanding speed, agility, balance, stamina and muscular endurance. Because of this it can only be played by those who are already fit.

Playing squash solo gives you the advantage of finding your own rhythm and technique and improving your fitness for the game in your own time. Playing squash with a partner, however, demands mental as well as physical agility as you have to assess, out-think and out-manoeuvre your opponent.

Squash makes large demands on the heart and lungs; they have to transport large amounts of oxygen to the active muscles and prevent a build up of their waste products. It also demands local muscle endurance; the muscles of the legs, stomach, back, arms and shoulders have to be able to work for long periods without tiring.

Squash demands strength and flexibility of the legs and back, so that you can drop, bend and twist for shots, and speed and agility of the legs and feet, with good footwork so that you can maintain balance, and a high degree of concentration. Unlike tennis, squash doesn't allow you time to change grips for different strokes, so the right grip must be maintained all the time and the wrist must be strong and flexible, to lift and allow the racket to strike the ball on centre from different angles.

In squash the key to winning is skilful volleying, and to do this you need concentration, stamina and speed, an ability to keep control of the ball and apply pressure on your opponent by quickening the game. Relaxation in action is also necessary in order to allow the arm and shoulder to make the smooth swing that precedes all well-played strokes.

Warming up and training

Squash demands that you are able to stretch, bend, twist, jump and turn more rapidly forwards, backwards and sideways. To avoid strains and injuries during the game and stiff muscles and joints after the game, warm-up and warm-down exercises are essential, and should always include static exercises for your legs, back, arms and shoulders.

If you want to be professional you should develop your own training programme, including exercises for endurance, agility and strength as well as static exercises for all-over flexibility and relaxation in action. Whatever your aspirations as a player, as squash is played indoors it is recommended that outdoor activities like jogging, running, sprinting and swimming be included in your training programme. Additionally, because squash is intense and competitive, it is recommended that other activities are enjoyed, albeit at a more leisurely pace.

▶ **Jahangir Khan v. Qamar Zaman, 1984**

Cricket

Although the words cricket, wicket and bat originate from the Anglo-Saxon, the earliest record of a game called 'Clykett' is from the mid-sixteenth century. Early writings show that, through the aristocracy and gentry, eighteenth-century cricket evolved from local village contests to organised games that were highly popular among all classes.

During this period the MCC (Marylebone Cricket Club) was formed, and by the 1800s Lords had been established. The first All-England Eleven was raised in 1850 and cricket rose further in popularity in the 1860s. This was partly due to the emergence of a magnificent player, W. G. Grace, a living legend and an original sporting hero.

Nowadays professional cricket is highly competitive, requiring a high degree of skill and physical fitness. International events such as test matches rank high among sporting entertainments.

Useful tips

Fundamentally the game consists of batting, bowling, fielding and wicket-keeping.

The skilful batsman can play a variety of different strokes, either defensive or attacking. However all strokes require the right grip, backlift and stance. The proper grip requires strength and flexibility of the wrists and hands. The hands should be properly aligned with each other, the top hand gripping firmly, with the right amount of bat exposed.

Without the right backlift, the batsman has little hope of either defending or attacking. From the backlift a defensive stroke is played but not followed through, the face of the bat being brought in line with the ball and angled to deflect it. In contrast an attacking stroke needs a full follow through for a really hard hit; a long high backlift gives the momentum to hit the ball harder. To develop a good backlift and stroke demands strength and flexibility in the arms and shoulders, and the easy rotation of the upper spine.

For the batsman, posture is all important in order to make full use of the body and to allow you to strike the ball squarely with your body-weight behind each stroke. The knees must remain slightly flexed, the spine straight, the head turned to see the ball and the shoulders in line with the bowler. Matches are often won by snatching quick runs between the wickets; if you are not to be run out, speed and agility are therefore vital.

Sound judgment, rhythm and coordination on the part of the bowler enables him to deliver the ball with the desired effect. Remember that only about 20 per cent of the speed of the ball comes from the speed of the delivery stride. Strength and flexibility of the arms and shoulders enables you to use a wide overarm swing with a strong high delivery, while dexterity of the hands and wrists improves the variety and speed of the various spins placed upon the ball while it is being delivered.

Fielding demands speed and precision and the ability to run fast, to catch or intercept and to throw with strength and accuracy. Catching, for example, requires balance, concentration and relaxation in action, especially in the arms and hands; often the fielder must catch a ball at speed, stretching and leaping for the ball, which takes coordination and agility. Throwing, too, requires strength and accuracy; often extreme speed and coor-

dination are needed to pick up a ball and throw it in one movement. For fielding at its best, each player must really specialise in a specific fielding position and must work in close coordination with the bowler.

And last but by no means least, the wicket-keeper requires an even higher level of mobility and concentration. To be able to catch, often at great speed, from the left or the right, to maintain a squatting position for long periods of time and to be able to move from this position with agility demands strength, flexibility and relaxation in action.

To maintain the skills and techniques and ensure that they do not break down under sustained pressure, every player needs to cultivate fitness. Warm-up exercises, including static exercises for the legs, spine, shoulders and hands, will do much to improve your game and help to prevent strains and injuries, while warm-down exercises must also be practised if you wish to avoid stiff muscles and joints.

To play your best, other sports like running and swimming, and a complete static exercise routine, should all be included in your regular training programme.

▶ **Ian Botham, England all-rounder, 1986**

Basketball

Dr James Naismith, a PE instructor from Springfield School, Massachusetts, developed basketball for his students in 1891. The game was an instant success and spread to Mexico before the end of that year. By 1897 a national college championship had started in the States and in 1898 the first professional league, the National Basketball League, was formed there.

In 1936 basketball became an Olympic sport and in the same year the Amateur Basketball Association was founded in England. However, the United States are world leaders in the game, having won more Olympic events than any other country. They were only beaten for the first time, by Russia, in the 1972 Munich Olympics.

Useful tips

Basketball involves an offensive game, played by the attacking team in possession of the ball, and the defensive game, played to defend the goal and recover the ball. Accurate passing and skilful dribbling are vital to good offensive play, and this calls for agility and flexibility.

The body's stance must be kept low and the ball must be kept between the knees and the waist in order to retain control and prevent a steal – in this position the player should be able to bounce the ball through and around the legs. The ball should be bounced like a yo-yo, maintaining contact with the whole hand. The flat of the fingers and the outside of the palm should be used and a fluid wrist movement should follow the ball through. When moving forward, the ball should be kept a step and a half in front of the body, and both hands should be used equally. The stance of the body is higher for this movement and the ball is bounced higher.

Passing the ball at precisely the right moment, at the right speed and at the right height takes coordination and concentration. Passes are made from the chest, overhead – just in front of the head to prevent a steal from behind – and on the bounce. Passing from the chest is made at close quarters, passing overhead is a high pass, and passing on the bounce is made to bypass an opponent. Other passes, made by really skilful players, include passes through the legs, from behind the back, a one-handed hook pass and a javelin pass.

Within scoring distance, control is crucial. The stance must be low in order to be able to move quickly to the left or right, and the body must be positioned between the ball and an opponent.

For shooting, the body should be facing the basket squarely with the feet, knees, hips, shoulders and head in line. The shoot requires the body-weight to be on the balls of the feet, crouched and ready to spring. With the head up and the eyes on the basket, the action itself launches the ball from around the forehead and the hands follow through for accuracy.

The lay-up shot is a relaxed movement made from under the basket, and requiring agility for a good jump; the body is stretched and you lay the ball in the net off the backboard. The jump shot is a distance shot requiring the player to jump high in the air and aim for the ring itself. The free throw is made from a crouch-to-tiptoe movement, while the hook shot is a specialised movement requiring flexibility in the hand, hooking the ball over the head into the basket.

Basketball involves running and sprinting, bending, jumping, twisting and stretching. To be good at the game you have to be agile and flexible; relaxation in action is important and speed, coordination and accuracy all add to the potential of a good player. And you must always remember that basketball is a team game; using other members of the team to beat an opponent contributes to your team's success and is a far better tactic than striving for personal achievement.

Warming up and training

Warm-up exercises for the legs, arms and spine will help avoid strains and injury while warm-down exercises should be practised if you want to avoid stiff muscles and joints after the game.

For a training programme, running, including sprints, and swimming can be combined with the regular practice of a static routine.

▶ **Lakers beat Celtics, Kareem shoots**

Baseball

Clyckett and stoolball were popular in medieval England and from these two games it seems that rounders was developed. During the seventeenth and eighteenth centuries rounders was taken to America by British immigrants and was then played as baseball and goalball.

In 1875 Alexander Cartwright brought order to the game and formalised some rules and field dimensions thereby laying the foundations for baseball as it is played today. Protective clothing was introduced by Tim Tyng of Boston in 1875, and by the mid-eighteen-eighties two major American baseball leagues had been established, the first the National League followed by the American League, while in England the British Baseball Federation was established in 1890.

Today baseball is played by some nineteen million Americans, it is highly popular in Canada and throughout South America; it is Japan's national game and South Korea's biggest spectator sport.

Currently, baseball is played in some eighty countries throughout the world and because of its increasing popularity it's thought that it will be included as a full medal sport in the 1992 Olympics.

▼ **Reggie Jackson**

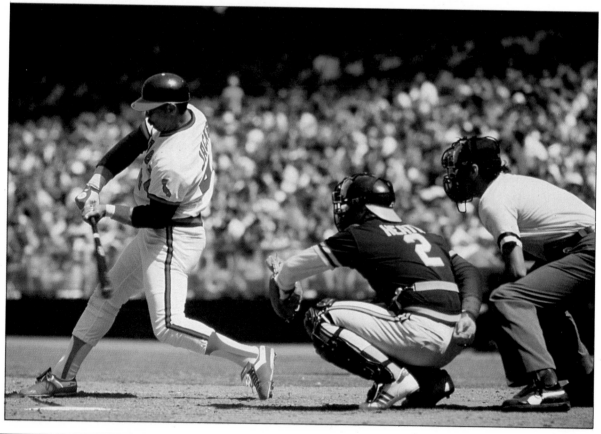

The pitch

A baseball field is fan shaped with a 90 foot diamond wedge marked from the apex. At each corner of the diamond, bases are marked counter clockwise as first, second and third base, and the home plate, from where the batsman starts and finishes. A left and a right foul line drawn from the home plate extends beyond the first and third base and is connected by a semi circle. The area within this fan is known as the infield and the area outside the semi circle is called the outfield.

The game

Baseball is played by two teams, each team consists of nine men and both teams take it in turn to bat and field. Each team has nine innings and there is no break and no set time limit for each game. Substitutes are allowed but no player is allowed back on field once they have left.

The pitcher starts the game and delivers the ball in a variety of skilful ways designed to outmanoeuvre the batter. The batter of the offensive team must then hit the ball and attempt to reach a base before the defending fielders can get the ball to that base. In this way a team advances its runners around the bases and back to home plate scoring runs.

The winner of the game is the team that scores the most runs, each run being a complete circuit of all the bases. The teams reverse roles when the batting team accumulates three outs and if after nine innings the score is even, extra innings are played to decide the winners.

Special skills

Pitching, batting and fielding all demand their own special skills plus speed, agility and co-ordination. The batter must react with split second timing adjusting his stance as he follows the flight of the ball, some being delivered at over 90 m.p.h.

The catcher, like a wicket keeper, remains in a squat position behind the batter, indicating to the pitcher where to place the ball, ready to move in any direction to catch the ball and throw it accurately to a baseman, second base being a throw of some 130 feet.

The fielder must be able to catch and throw accurately, and to sprint and leap for the ball. The pitcher and batter must maintain flexibility in their arms and shoulders and back, as these areas are especially prone to injury. Runners and fielders must be relaxed during play if the impacts of diving or sliding for a ball or a base are to pass through the body. The successful player cultivates strength, stamina and flexibility through a comprehensive fitness programme as well as using warm up, and warm down, routines plus individual skills and techniques. For those who play, or wish to play for fun, combined with a static exercise programme, baseball and softball are an enjoyable and effective way to maintain and improve fitness. For the uninitiated, softball is the easier game and a good way to approach baseball.

American Football

American football is said to originate from medieval football, a game that was played in England during the middle ages, by any amount of people in a variety of disorganised ways.

Known as 'new rugby' it was played and developed at Harvard, Princetown and Yale until innovations that changed the game were introduced in the late nineteenth century. Walter C. Camp, a famous Yale half back, introduced these innovations and as a result the game became highly popular and Camp was acclaimed the father of 'Gridiron' or American football. In the early twentieth century the present scoring system was accepted and protective clothing made its appearance.

There are many great contributors to the game as it is played today and these include Heisman, a proponent of the forward pass, and Stagg, a remarkable player and coach, who introduced a number of brilliant defensive tactics. In the nineteen-twenties under the leadership of Joseph Carr, the National Football League was developed and professional football then became organised.

In England there are currently forty-eight teams in the British American Football League and the game is played in most European countries.

In America thirteen million spectators watched the two hundred and twenty-four regular season games throughout 1985, some sixty thousand people a game. The ten playoff games attracted nearly three quarters of a million spectators and the Super Bowl Final a crowd of seventy-four thousand.

The basics
An American football field is 120 yards long and 160 feet wide. It is sectioned to give each team 50 yards of territory from the midfield strip to the goal line, with an end zone of ten yards. The goal itself is situated in the end zone behind the goal line and from the goal line to the midfield, striped lines are drawn at intervals of every five yards. *The time period* for each game is one hour, which is divided into four 15-minute periods, with a fifteen-minute interval at half time, and extra time in the event of a draw.

◀ **Walter Payton, Chicago Bears**

The players
The game requires two teams, each team having eleven players on field with an unlimited number of substitutes that can be made between plays.

Scoring
This is made primarily by touching the ball down in the opposing team's end zone, kicking the ball over the crossbar between the goal posts and tackling or safety scoring in the end zones.

Playing
Progress is made across the yard lines towards the opponents' goal starting from a line of scrimmage by the offensive team, while the defending team try to prevent them from gaining yards. When the opposing team is tackled or goes out of bounds a new line of scrimmage is formed.

Special considerations
There are a number of common team strategies, tactics and techniques but basic play includes running or sprinting, blocking and tackling, catching and passing and kicking and jumping. American football is not the kind of game you play to get in shape. Serious players maintain a rigorous fitness programme all year round often combining extremes like karate and ballet to sharpen reflexes and maintain agility. For the professional, diet is important and together with a fitness programme mental conditioning also takes place.

Static exercises and relaxation techniques are also included in this programme to balance cultivated strength with suppleness and flexibility. Warm-up and warm-down exercises are used to continue relaxation in action and prevent soreness after a strenuous game.

Running, sprinting, blocking and tackling all require strength, stamina and suppleness while kicking and passing also demands the accuracy and coordination that comes with a balanced body. This is definitely a game that should not be played with stiff joints, as suppleness and flexibility will not only considerably reduce the risks and effects of injury but they will also greatly increase the skill of the player.

Injuries During Exercise

This chapter describes damage that can occur to joints and muscles during exercise, and how you can best treat such complaints.

Ligaments

Ligaments are tough fibrous bands that hold your bones together at the joints and stop them from extending beyond their normal range of movement. Most joints are supported by several bands of ligaments that take the strain from all directions.

Sprains and tears are the most common forms of injury to ligaments, usually caused by sudden violent over-extension of the joint, such as when you twist an ankle or knee. If such an injury occurs you can usually tell how bad it is by the size of the swelling; with a mild sprain the swelling is slight, but a severe strain can cause considerable swelling and is very painful.

Method of treatment

A mild sprain can just be bandaged, and a return to normal activity can be expected within a few days.

With a more severe sprain, crush some ice into a plastic bag, wrap the bag in a thin towel and place it over the injury for about 15 minutes. This will control the swelling and aid the healing process – and it feels good. After this, bandage the injury firmly, using a crepe bandage and making sure that you cover the area well. Try to keep the affected part (leg or arm) raised when resting, and repeat the treatment every three hours for 24 to 48 hours, depending on the extent of the injury.

With a severe sprain do not try to move the joint until the pain, swelling, discolouration, heat or numbness have lessened. Once this has happened, slowly move the joint and then *gently* try out the relevant static exercise or man-ipulation, combining this with self-massage until full movement has been restored. Do not return to full activity until the damage to the joint has fully healed.

If the ligament is ruptured or severed, prompt medical treatment is necessary and effective, but immediate first aid can be given while awaiting treatment.

Cramps and spasms

Cramps and spasms arise in the muscles as a result of physical injury, over-use (how many footballers have you seen convulsed with cramp?) and acute mental stress. They are spontaneous reflexes that reduce movement in order to impose rest and prevent further injury. Spasms in the limbs and lower back are most common as a result of misuse, over-use and injury, while spasms in the neck and abdomen are usually due to emotional stress.

During pain or acute stress, muscles do not tighten and relax in the normal way but remain in a constant state of semi-contraction. Because the muscle fibres cannot relax, the blood cannot flow freely through them and remove chemical waste products or bring oxygen and nutrients to them to allow the muscles to work normally. This state of tension wrecks the muscles and gives rise to pain, which in turn produces more tension, and so on.

Sometimes if the cramp or spasm is acute the muscle fibres tighten to such a degree that they form tiny knots that feel very tender when you press the muscle.

Method of treatment

Rest, heat and massage are the most immediate forms of treatment. A hot bath or a hot water bottle encourage the muscle to relax and then a gentle massage should begin to restore movement. When relaxation and movement has been restored, gentle stretching exercises will help the muscle restore its proper state of relaxation.

Muscles

Muscles pass across the joints, which they move and help to support. They consist of long bundles of fibres enclosed within sheaths and are attached to the bones by tendons.

Sprains and strains

Sprains and strains can occur when a muscle tightens too strongly or too quickly or is suddenly overstretched. This causes a sharp pain, followed by swelling, stiffness, tenderness and aching. The muscle is weakened and the condition is aggravated by use.

Bruising occurs as a result of a direct blow or knock against the muscle, or a fracture. Both cause damage inside the muscle and bleeding into the surrounding tissues, and bruising shows when the blood flow reaches the surface, although sometimes it is contained within the muscle.

Method of treatment

The immediate application of an ice pack and, where possible, a firm crepe bandage will help reduce the flow of blood and fluid into the muscle. This should be repeated every two to three hours while the injury subsides. Keep the affected part raised and, as the pain gets less, tighten and relax the muscle without movement.

As soon as the symptoms of injury have gone, *gently* stretch the muscle by applying the appropriate static exercise or manipulation and self-massage. Do not return to dynamic exercise until pain and stiffness have gone and the muscle is functioning well.

Inflammation

Inflammations of the muscles, tendons and joints are mostly caused by over-use and misuse. These conditions are usually extremely painful, swelling develops and the affected part often feels 'hot'. It is best *not* to try to exercise any muscles or joints that are badly swollen, inflamed, discoloured, locked or extremely painful. Under these conditions consult a recommended osteopath, chiropractor or physiotherapist.

Recovery
If you rest for too long or don't treat the injury, resistance to movement increases and, because of this, trying to get the muscle or joint to work again can take far longer and be more painful. Consequently the prompt use of appropriate exercises when the symptoms of injury have gone will increase your chances of a rapid and complete recovery.

The exercises must be performed regularly and carefully in order to extend the boundaries of movement and endurance *gradually*. However, take care not to over-stretch or over-contract the muscles or joint during recovery as this will actually slow down your progress.

Appendix I
Further reading

Baseball, Richard Saul Wurman (Access Press)

Basketball: Techniques, teaching and training, Brian Coleman (Kaye and Ward)

Bodylife, Arthur Balaskas (Sidgwick & Jackson)

The Complete American Football Book, Nicky Horne (Robson Books)

The Complete Book of Gymnastics, David Hunn (Ward Lock)

The Complete Book of Running, James Fixx (Chatto & Windus)

The Complete Book of Squash, Heather McKay (Angus and Robertson)

The Complete Guide to Running, Harry Wilson *et al.* (Sterling Publishing Co.)

The Cyclist's Manual, Doug Colligan & Dick Tercsi (Sterling Publishing Co.)

Enjoying Skating, The Diagram Group (Paddington Press)

Enjoying Soccer, The Diagram Group (Paddington Press)

Football, Tom Tully (Beaver Books)

Going Skiing, ed. Michael Smee & Frank Warwick (BBC Publications)

A Guide to American Football, Ken Thomas (Orbis and Channel 4)

A Guide To Baseball, Andrew Thomas (Macdonald & Co.)

Recover Quickly, Susan Hooker (Unwin Paperbacks)

The Handbook of Tennis, Paul Douglas (Pelham Books)

The New Cyclist, Tony Osman (Collins)

New Wave Roller Skating, Bruce Samford (Piccolo Books)

Light on Yoga, B. K. S. Iyengar (Unwin Paperbacks)

The Science of Swimming, James E. Counsilman (Pelham Books)

Skateway, Robert Cousins (Hutchinson)

Skills and Tactics of Tennis, Tony Mottram (Marshall Cavendish Books)

Ski: The Expertsman, Honore Banner & Gerald Munrois (Newnes)

Soft Exercise, Arthur Balaskas & John Stirk (Unwin Paperbacks)

Squash, John Taylor (Pelham Books)

Start Well, Michael & Inke Schwarts (Pagoda Books)

Tai-Chi, Cheng Man Ch'ing & Robert W. Smith (Tuttle)

The Way of the Warrior, Howard Reid & Michael Croucher (Century Publishing Co.)

Weight Training, E. G. Bartlett (David & Charles)

Yoga, Mircea Ileade (Routledge & Kegan Paul)

The Young Player's Guide to Cricket, Derek Randall (David & Charles)

Appendix 2
Useful Addresses

**The Sports Council
Information Centre
16 Upper Woburn Place
London WC1H 0PQ
Tel: 01 388 1277**

ATHLETICS

Amateur Athletic Association &
Women's Amateur Athletic
Association
Francis House
Francis Street
London SW1P 1DL
Tel: 01 828 9326/4731

BADMINTON

Badminton Association of England
National Badminton Centre
Bradwell Road
Loughton Lodge
Milton Keynes
Buckinghamshire MK8 9LA
Tel: Milton Keynes (0908) 568 822

BASEBALL

British Amateur Baseball and
Softball Federation
197 Newbridge Road
Hull
North Humberside HU9 2LR
Tel: Hull (0482) 76169

BASKETBALL

English Basket Ball Association
Calomax House
Lupton Avenue
Leeds LS9 7EE
Tel: Leeds (0532) 496 044

CRICKET

National Cricket Association
Lord's Cricket Ground
London NW8 8QN
Tel: 01 289 6098

Women's Cricket Association
16 Upper Woburn Place
London WC1H 0QF
Tel: 01 387 3423

CYCLING

British Cycling Federation
16 Upper Woburn Place
London WC1H 0QE
Tel: 01 387 9320

Cyclist's Touring Club
Cotterell House
69 Meadrow
Godalming
Surrey GU7 7HS
Tel: Godalming (048 68) 7217/8

FOOTBALL

American Football Association
21 Belmont Avenue
Struden Park
Bournemouth
Dorset
Tel: Bournemouth (0202) 510 411

Budweiser American Football
League
30–35 Drury Lane
London WC2 B5RH
Tel: 01 379 3480

JOGGING

National Jogging Association
Newstead Abbey Park
Newstead
Nottinghamshire
Tel: Mansfield (0623) 793 496

GYMNASTICS

British Amateur Gymnastics
Association
2 Buckingham Avenue East
Slough
Berkshire SL1 3EA
Tel: Slough (75) 32763

SKATING

National Skating Association of
Great Britain
15–27 Gee Street
London WC1V 2RU
Tel: 01 253 3824

SKI-ING

British Ski Federation
118 Eaton Square
London SW1W 9AF
Tel: 01 235 8227/8

English Ski Council
4th Floor
Area Library Building
The Precinct
Halesowen
West Midlands B63 4AJ
Tel: Birmingham (021) 501 2314

SQUASH

Squash Rackets Association
Francis House
Francis Street
London SW1P 1DE
Tel: 01 828 3064/6

Women's Squash Rackets
Association
345 Upper Richmond Road West
Sheen
London SW14 8QN
Tel: 01 876 6219

SWIMMING

Amateur Swimming Association
Harold Fern House
Derby Square
Loughborough
Leicestershire LE11 0AL
Tel: Loughborough (0509) 230 431

TENNIS

Tennis and Rackets Associations
c/o The Queen's Club
Palliser Road
London W14 9EQ
Tel: 01 381 4746

Lawn Tennis Association
Barons Court
West Kensington
London W14 9EG
Tel: 01 385 2366

WEIGHT LIFTING

British Amateur Weight Lifters'
Association
3 Iffley Turn
Oxford
Tel: Oxford (0865) 778 319

YOGA

British Wheel of Yoga
Grafton Grange
Grafton
York YO5 9QQ
Tel: Boroughbridge (090 12) 3386